Affluent *for* Life

13 Wealth Management Issues to Protect You and Your Family

TED RIDLEHUBER

Charter Financial Publishing Network • Shrewsbury, NJ

Charter Financial Publishing Network
Shrewsbury, NJ 07702
(732) 450-8866
(732) 450-8877 (fax)
www.fa-mag.com

For information on special discounts for bulk purchases, please contact Charter Financial Publishing Network at (732) 450-8866, ext. 207.

This book is sold with the understanding that the subject matter covered does not constitute legal, tax or other professional planning advice for any specific individual or situation. Anyone planning to take any action in any of the areas described by this book should, of course, seek professional advice from qualified accountants, lawyers, tax and other advisors who can review your specific needs and circumstances and determine if any planning strategy or action is appropriate for you.

ISBN 0-9766574-1-4

Library of Congress Control Number: 2006922035

Designed by Pamela Terry, Opus 1 Design, www.Opus1Design.com

Printed in the United States of America, April 2006

To my wife, Caroline,
and my three daughters,
Alice Ann, Susan and Amy,
whose deep love and support
made this book possible.

CONTENTS

ACKNOWLEDGEMENTS

Over the last 35 years, I have worked with numerous families on their wealth management plans. This book is the result of my experiences with them, and of my concern that so many families do not do the planning they should to protect their assets and their descendents' futures. The reason most people procrastinate is that they are overwhelmed by the complexity of the task.

In this book I have simplified and organized the process using 13 clearly outlined steps that any reader can follow. This book would have been impossible without the help of the following friends, colleagues and family members:

Verner F. Chaffin, Callaway Professor Emeritus, University of Georgia Law School, who first excited me about providing wealth management planning for families.

William E. Barrett, my first partner at Cannon Financial Institute, Inc., whose courage supported me in expanding nationwide with assistance to families in wealth management planning.

Roy Adams, Attorney-At-Law, whose generosity in sharing his experiences working with wealthy families has broadened my knowledge.

Marc Myers, whose editorial help on this book was invaluable.

The many wealth management professionals whose confidence in me has allowed me to work not only with their employees but also with a myriad of their wealthy clients.

My dedicated colleagues at Cannon Financial Institute, Inc., who support me daily in uncounted ways and without whom this book would not have been written.

My three daughters, Alice Ann, Susan and Amy, whose sacrifices and understanding gave me time to work with families nationwide. Their gifts of five grandchildren made the urgency of family wealth management planning very personal to me.

My wife, Caroline, my best critic, whose love and support have enabled me to commit the time and energy to gain the experience and knowledge to construct the wealth management process contained in this book.

INTRODUCTION

On June 3, 1962, a chartered passenger jet cleared for takeoff began accelerating down Runway 8 at Orly Airport in Paris. When the plane reached maximum ground speed, the nose started to rise off the tarmac. But a failed motor in a wing kept the body on the ground. The pilot instantly realized the seriousness of the problem and tried to abort the takeoff by breaking hard. But too little runway remained. Unable to stop in time, the plane skidded across an access road, clipped a set of landing lights and rammed into a stone cottage, exploding in flames. A total of 130 passengers and crew died that day. Only two stewardesses sitting in the plane's rear survived when the tail broke off just before impact. It was the second-worst passenger-jet crash in aviation history at the time.

When news of the crash reached Atlanta, the city went into shock. On board were 106 members of the Atlanta Art Association returning from a month-long trip to Europe. The group had visited all the great museums and had purchased artwork, antiques and artifacts for private collections and generous gifts to Atlanta institutions. In an instant, most of Atlanta's wealthiest art patrons and spouses had perished, leaving behind 33 children and young adults orphaned by the disaster.

Writing about this event today brings back heartbreaking memories for me. In June 1962, I had just graduated from the University of Georgia Law School, and within hours of the air disaster I was recruited by an Atlanta bank to work with the settlement of the estates actuated by the disaster. Many of the wealthy people who had died that day had named a spouse as executor of their will, but in most cases both spouses had been killed. Many of the couples had named a bank trust department to be contingent trustee as a fallback. The problem was that many couples had not updated their wills in prior years and their estates had become much larger since then. They also had not accounted for all tax-saving opportunities, or prepared their plans so descendents could manage the taxes that would be owed.

Over the next five years, the bank and I worked closely with about 20 children of the crash victims and their next of kin, helping them gain control of family assets and settle tax obligations. We also helped them manage their assets and the sizable sums from the suit settlements that followed. To this day I still recall the profound grief those children and their relatives felt. The experience for me was deeply moving and eye-opening: I learned firsthand that no matter how wealthy and careful you are, unpredictable events can change everything for your family in a flash. I also realized that without sound wealth-management plans in place, the fortune you amass over a lifetime can be squandered if the wealth winds up in inexperienced hands.

A few years ago I ran into some of the children I helped back in the early 1960s. They're adults now, of course, but talking to them reminded me that the single biggest financial challenge facing wealthy people today is preserving family fortunes for future generations. Most wealthy families know this only too well: In a recent study, the top 1% of wealthy Americans said that avoiding financial obstacles for the next generation was their No. 1 concern—ahead of all other issues including terrorism, which was No. 2.

Yet only a few wealthy families take steps necessary to ensure that their fortunes will thrive and survive future generations. We know that a family business often is the primary source of family wealth. Yet only 5% of the wealth created by family businesses lasts beyond the third generation, according to another recent study. That means chances are slim that your lifetime of hard work will do your grandkids or great grandkids a lick of good.

And that's a shame. Wealth erosion is not genetic or inevitable. In my experience, wealth disappears over time because wealth creators don't plan properly for generational wealth succession. Wealth creators are especially good at capitalizing on business opportunities and parlaying risks into fortunes. But the drive required to build a business often comes with hubris and control issues that can fuel family conflicts and lead to errors in financial judgment. It's not surprising that many wealth creators become estranged from some or all of their children. Or that some fail to engage heirs and train them early in financial matters or the family business. Or that others believe that financial risk is best reduced by spreading assets and advisory tasks among different financial institutions and brokers.

Making peace with children to sustain family fortunes over generations is far more productive than treating them with contempt or pointing out their shortcomings. Educating heirs about the family business and finances is far more enduring than just setting up trusts. And concentrating all of your finances with a single wealth manager or team can do more to grow and preserve wealth than dividing assets and responsibilities among many different professionals who don't communicate with each other or know your complete financial picture.

I've never met a wealth creator who said that he or she wanted future family members to live in poverty. Plenty have said they wished heirs would work harder, become focused or stop abusing drugs and alcohol. But in all my years working as an advisor to high-net-worth families, I've never met a single wealth creator who didn't think daily about the best way to leave a positive mark on society while alive, make heirs happy and sustain fortunes for years after they're gone.

That's why I wrote this book. I have found that wealthy families, like all families today, are time-squeezed and often unsure how best to achieve financial goals. For example, estate planning alone is not a wealth-succession plan and won't do much to prevent a *shirt sleeves to shirt sleeves* scenario from unfolding. That's where the working stiff in shirt sleeves who made the fortune hands off wealth to irresponsible heirs who mismanage their inheritance and wind up in shirt sleeves, just like the wealth creator on his way up.

Keeping wealth in the family is not nearly as difficult as many advisors would lead you to believe. I have compressed the issues that families like yours will face to as few a number as I can, and I arrived at 13. Why 13? I simply couldn't get the number any lower, and 12 weren't enough. These 13 principles cover wealth expansion, wealth protection and wealth preservation. I also will show you why it's essential to hire a wealth manager who oversees your entire financial universe and how best to choose one.

All 13 principles are important because over time, the threats to your family's fortune will certainly rise. I don't know about you, but I can't name too many wealthy decedents of 19th century railroad magnates or early 20th century retail moguls. That's because over generations, families expand. Children have children and their children have children, and the sad truth is most will have little interest in the family business or finance. Many will prefer to go their own way. Others will prefer to spend rather than save. Over time, wealth can become so diluted among so many disinterested heirs that less and less remains for future generations.

But what if you could take steps now to reduce the odds of that happening? What if you could enjoy your wealth within reason, allow your children to enjoy your wealth, and ensure that future generations would expand, protect and preserve what's left so that they could not only enjoy it but also take steps to preserve it?

Back in 1962, I had no idea I would be spending so many years of my life helping wealthy families plan not only for the future of their families but also the future of future family members they will never meet. But life's random events leave deep impressions and often give us purpose. I've acted on all 13 principles for my family and future generations, so I know they'll work for you.

If you cherish your family, as I know you do, implementing these principles will ensure that your life's work will be appreciated for a long time to come.

1

INVESTING FOR WEALTH EXPANSION AND PROTECTION

Like most affluent people, you probably have two big wishes for your invested wealth: You want your portfolio to grow steadily over time so it can support your family's lifestyle—and you want your portfolio protected against downside risk so you can pass as much of your wealth as possible to heirs and charitable causes.

Yet many affluent investors I talk to during my travels around the country do not have a single, comprehensive plan for maximizing portfolio returns or minimizing the impact of market declines. Instead, they prefer to maintain multiple portfolios at several different investment firms. When I ask them why they've chosen this strategy, they tell me they aren't comfortable putting all their eggs in one basket. When I ask why they don't at least have one wealth advisor overseeing all of their assets, they tell me they would rather manage risk by diversifying among several different advisors and firms.

Most people are surprised when I tell them that investing this way doesn't lower risk but actually raises it. When multiple brokers or advisors are familiar with only a fraction of your wealth, their investment recommendations will be limited to just the universe they manage, and your overall portfolio will likely suffer. Advisors who operate independently of each other will be unaware of your total portfolio and cannot possibly recommend a mix of assets that protects your wealth and family over the long term.

By comparison, if you hire one wealth advisor who works for a firm with an *open architecture*—meaning the advisor is not limited to only proprietary funds and managers but is able to buy any investment, fund or manager—you are more likely to own a more diversified portfolio that experiences less volatility. Why? Because one wealth advisor will be better able to manage the two biggest threats to your portfolio—an inappropriate asset allocation and unwanted overlap and conflicts—as well as having appropriate checks and balances among the investments, funds and managers you own.

To achieve your long-term investment goals—wealth expansion, wealth protection and wealth preservation—your portfolio will need an asset allocation that takes into consideration your current situation, your future, your feelings and your family dynamics. You also will need to be sure the investments for those allocations correlate well with each other and don't result in redundancies.

In this chapter, I will explain how to select the right asset allocation and manage it on an ongoing basis by rebalancing and reallocating. I also will explain how to make sure your investments, funds and managers are individually and collectively excellent. These strategies will lower your portfolio's exposure to risk and help your wealth grow over time.

Structuring Your Asset Allocation

Choosing an asset allocation that positions your portfolio for growth and limits the threats to its value isn't hard. I have devoted my life to simplifying this process. Why is asset allocation so important? No one can predict which investments will do well over the next 12 months and which will do poorly. It's also impossible to predict which investments doing poorly now will suddenly do well, and which investments performing well will suddenly suffer setbacks. You also can't predict how long investments will do well or poorly. All of this uncertainty is known as *risk*.

To reduce the impact of uncertainty, your portfolio's assets need to be allocated among many different types of equity (real estate and stocks) and fixed-income (bonds) positions. But selecting an asset allocation that will meet your financial needs can be tricky. Some people mistakenly hold too large a percentage of their portfolio's total value in real estate investments because property values may be surging. Other people hold too large an allocation of stocks because they may have been told that the stock market always goes up over time. While historically that's true—the stock market has increased significantly in value over extensive periods of time, such as 50 years or longer—stocks can remain flat or even decline over 10-year periods. For example, between 1964 and 1974, the S&P 500 actually went down—from 84.75 to 68.56. There are no sure things in real estate, stocks or any investment whose value is determined by an open market. What goes up often goes down, and tomorrow's sudden events can dramatically affect one or more parts of your investment portfolio.

Smart *asset allocation* is about diversifying your portfolio among a carefully chosen mix of investments based on your current situation, your future, your feelings and your family dynamics. When properly structured, this mix will give your total portfolio an opportunity to profit when some of its assets soar in value while at the same time preventing your portfolio from taking too bad a hit when some of its assets drop in value. In other words, your risk is strategically spread out—giving you overall exposure to investment surges while limiting your exposure to investment plunges.

When you and your wealth advisor sit down to structure an asset allocation, in addition to spreading assets among different investment categories—equity (stocks and real estate), fixed income (bonds) and cash—you also will diversify among different investment classes within each category. So on the equity side of your portfolio, you will be invested in a range of different types of stocks based on company size (large, medium and small), investment style (growth and value) and sectors (healthcare, technology, energy and others).

What's the best way to determine your asset allocation? When you and your wealth advisor determine how your portfolio should be allocated, four factors should be considered—your current situation, your future, your feelings and your family dynamics. Let's look at each one:

1. **Your current situation.** What do you need your portfolio to do for you now? Some people need cash flow to fund their retirement or to pay medical expenses for children or grandchildren. Other people may not need any income at all.

2. **Your future.** What events in your future will need to be funded by your portfolio's assets? These events may range from paying for a child or grandchild's education to the need for retirement income. Personally, I like the word *future* because it implies

more than just goals, which are often thought of only as the good things you plan to experience. By thinking in terms of *future events*, you will be compelled to think about not only the good things but also the unknown or unfortunate events you are likely to face, such as rising health expenses or care for children. To help you start to think about your future needs and their impact on your asset allocation, ask yourself the following questions:

> ➤ What events in the future will likely require cash outlays?

> ➤ What will be the magnitude of these events? For example, if you expect you'll be asked to help pay for private school for a grandchild, what's the projected cost likely to be over those academic years?

> ➤ What is the probability that these events will occur?

> ➤ When will the cash be needed? In other words, how soon will you have to write a check?

3. **Your feelings.** Feelings are your emotions, and emotions drive behavior. For instance, how you feel about risk is typically based on your emotional reactions to recent events. When you hear, see or read about an investment opportunity, for example, your emotions are stirred up and you feel an urge to react. Sometimes your feelings can be so strong that they cloud rational thought and convince you to take impulsive actions you may later regret. For instance, you may have read about a hot investment and feel that if you don't act fast, that investment opportunity will pass and you will miss out on a spectacular gain—even though acting quickly is rarely necessary or prudent.

Even the wisest, wealthiest individuals make investment decisions based on feelings. If the stock market is way down, your feelings often tell you to dump all of your stocks. When real estate values are soaring and everyone is in Florida buying a condominium, your feelings may tell you to start calling Palm Beach realtors. When creating your asset allocation, you and your wealth advisor must consider your feelings, especially when it comes to risk and how much you believe you can truly tolerate—without overestimating your risk exposure.

When most people try to manage their portfolio's asset allocation on their own, they almost always overweight their feelings. I recently worked with a retired couple in Northern California in their late 50s. In 1998, they had just sold their clothing-store business for about $8 million. While at a party hosted by a neighbor back then, the couple listened as their host—who was half their age—remarked that his family's portfolio was up 48% thanks to an 80% concentration in large-cap technology growth stocks. Later on, when the couple found themselves alone at the party, they wondered aloud why their portfolio was up only 20%.

The next day, the husband called the three brokers who managed different parts of his and his wife's assets. He instructed each of them to load up on the types of stocks owned by his younger neighbor. So the brokers all bought large-cap technology growth stocks. But before you condemn these brokers as reckless, given the couple's retirement age, you should know that the brokers were all, in fact, good, honest professionals. They simply were under the assumption they were handling only the aggressive segment of the older retiree's complete portfolio. The retiree had kept each broker in the dark about the others.

Within a short period of time, the older couple's portfolio did indeed start to rise rapidly. That is until March 2000, when the stock market started its steep slide downward, and large-cap technology growth stocks suffered. By year-end, the older couple's portfolio tumbled 60%—an especially devastating drop for this couple. They were counting on their total portfolio to generate income for living expenses and to help pay for their grandchildren's college educations.

I started working with the couple to repair their portfolio in 2003. Today their assets can cover their annual expenses, which of course had to be lowered following the collapse of their portfolio in 2000. Their standard of living is now slightly lower, and completely funding several college educations is out. But they don't have to deplete their portfolio's principal, which would have been disastrous. When I look back, I am still amazed that the source of the couple's portfolio troubles originated from a casual conversation with a neighbor who may or may not have been entirely truthful. That conversation at the party was enough to stir their emotions and feelings.

As you can see, feelings have no place in investment decisions without giving equal weighting to your current situation, future needs and family dynamics. Working with a trusted wealth advisor to structure your asset allocation ensures that your feelings will play a role in determining the composition of your portfolio, but will not overshadow your objectives. You may hear about a great oil refinery stock or that real estate is about to tank and then feel you need to take action. But if you have a trusted wealth advisor and an appropriate asset allocation, your feelings will be pushed aside by rational thought and you are more likely to stay the course originally selected.

4. **Your family dynamics.** Your asset allocation will take into account your family's size, relationship and the needs of individual family members. Your asset allocation should be altered only when your lifestyle changes or your family changes. You may have created your original allocation when your children were young. But many years later, your children's needs may have changed dramatically. One may be in college while the other may have just given birth to your grandchild. I guarantee that your children's financial needs in this situation will be very different from when they were young. As your family changes your allocation will likely have to change as well, to meet your changing financial needs.

Once you and your wealth advisor have determined the right asset mix for you based on these four factors, your allocation should not change unless one or more of these factors changes significantly, such as you retire. This asset-allocation modification is called *reallocating*. Otherwise, your allocations should remain constant. This means that if you and your wealth advisor decide to invest 30% in stocks, 30% in real estate, 30% in bonds and 10% in cash, those allocations should always remain in force until that asset allocation is no longer appropriate for you.

MONITORING YOUR ASSET ALLOCATION

Asset-allocation management is not a static process. You can't just select an allocation and forget about it. Think of your portfolio as a perfectly round pie. Changes in the market can push your pie out of shape as certain assets in your allocation expand while others shrink. Steps must be taken to bring your pie back to its original shape. This step is called *rebalancing*. Otherwise, your portfolio's exposure to downside risk will rise.

As efficient as a customized asset allocation is in reducing portfolio risk, it is not a one-time event, and your allocation must be monitored carefully. Different investments go up and down at different points in time. For example, in just one year or less, large-cap value stocks may be up significantly in value while international stocks may be down. When different investments rise and fall in value, the value of your holdings in those assets will likely go up and down as well, and your portfolio may no longer be allocated appropriately. For example, you may have originally decided to hold 60% of your portfolio in stocks, 20% in fixed income and 20% in cash. But if the stock funds you hold climb significantly in value to a point where they make up 72% of your portfolio's value, your fixed income and cash allocations will make up only 14% each.

The way to remedy the distortion in your portfolio is to *rebalance*—which simply means to take steps to restore your portfolio to its original allocation. There are two ways to rebalance:

1. You can sell shares in investments that have exceeded their original allocations and invest the proceeds in assets that have dropped below their allocation levels.

2. Or you can invest new money in assets that have dropped below their preset allocations.

If we were to use the first method to rebalance the portfolio in our earlier example, we would sell stocks to return the equity allocation to 60% of the portfolio and invest the proceeds in fixed-income investments and cash equivalents to bring each up to its original 20% allocation. If we were to use the second method, we would invest new money in fixed income and cash to restore the portfolio's original 60%/20%/20% allocation.

The method you choose will often have to do with whether the assets in question are in your taxable or tax-deferred account. Selling assets and using the proceeds to rebalance clearly is more tax-efficient in an Individual Retirement Account (IRA), 401(k), Simplified Employee Pension (SEP) and other tax-deferred accounts than in a taxable account, where you'll likely owe taxes on the realized gains. Rebalancing by investing new money in allocations that have underperformed makes more sense in taxable accounts.

While rebalancing sounds simple enough, most investors balk when it's time to do so. Why? They let their feelings get in the way. Emotionally, investors are reluctant to sell top-performing assets or invest in assets that are doing poorly. Their instinct tells them to buy more of their winning assets and dump their losers. Rebalancing, as you can see, is somewhat counterintuitive. You're selling the assets delivering the strongest returns in favor of the laggards. It just doesn't feel right. To keep your feelings out of the rebalancing equation, you and your wealth advisor need to come up with a disciplined, unemotional rebalancing approach that rebalances automatically when certain criteria are met. In the case of my family's portfolio, my wife and I have authorized our wealth advisor to rebalance any time the value of an asset category (stocks, bonds or cash) rises or falls 10% from our chosen allocation.

Over time, rebalancing has big rewards. For one, a rebalanced portfolio is more likely to outperform a similarly allocated buy-and-hold portfolio. For another, it's likely to be much less volatile. The lessons here are simple: Rebalance when the market changes, reallocate when your current situation, future, feelings or family dynamics change. And be sure you have a disciplined rebalancing process based on agreed-upon deviations—10% in my personal situation—to prevent your feelings from getting in the way of what's necessary. A disciplined rebalancing process will override your feelings by selling your allocation's gainers and investing in allocations that are down.

CORRELATION OF INVESTMENTS, FUNDS AND MANAGERS

A second risk to your portfolio is a poor correlation between your investments, funds and managers. Even if you create the perfect asset allocation for your needs, rebalance when your portfolio is no longer allocated the way you structured it, and reallocate when the allocation is no longer appropriate based on your current needs, future needs, feelings and family dynamics, there's still one more step: You need to be sure that the investments, funds and managers selected for your portfolio do not excessively overlap nor excessively conflict.

Owning a portfolio of excellent investments, funds and managers isn't enough. You and your wealth advisor have to make sure that each investment in your portfolio correlates or interrelates appropriately with the other investments, funds and managers in your portfolio, so your whole portfolio is as good as its parts. For example, you may own six excellent mutual funds. But if five of the six funds own the same 10 stocks, your assets may not be as well allocated as you think.

Two criteria should be used by your wealth advisor when selecting and retaining investments, funds and managers for your portfolio:

1. Each investment, fund or manager must stand alone as being excellent.

2. Each investment, fund or manager must also interrelate appropriately with the other investment funds or managers in your portfolio.

When your portfolio's assets are managed by different firms, there is going to be greater risk in how the investments, funds and managers interrelate. When I look at a new client's portfolios, I often have no problem with the investments, funds or managers individually. But I will often have a problem with the whole portfolio. Typically, I will see overlap when I dissect the funds they own. So even though a fund may have *large-cap value* in its name, that fund may own a large stake in the same five stocks as a fund with the word *balanced* in its name. Or I may see a portfolio that owns a fund whose manager is selling stocks that another fund manager in the portfolio is buying.

When this happens, I tell clients that they have an interesting phenomenon going on. "You're selling to yourself," I tell them. Their typical response is, "We had no idea."

Creating a portfolio with assets that are well correlated and interrelated isn't always about selecting the best managers you can find. How the investments, funds and managers work together as a team in your portfolio is much more significant. The importance of teamwork is perhaps best illustrated by the 1980 Olympic hockey team. When the U.S. Olympic Hockey Committee hired Herb Brooks to be the team's coach, it asked him to assemble a team of 20 from the 100 or so top amateur hockey players invited to try out in Colorado Springs. Remember, back in 1980 you had to be an amateur to play in the Olympics.

Instead of selecting the top two superstars, Brooks cut them first from his list during the tryout rounds. The U.S. Olympic Hockey Committee was stunned by Brooks' move, and insisted that these players had to be included if the team was to stand a chance at beating the Russians. Brooks refused, saying he was hired to put together a winning team, and that this required the players who worked well together, not necessarily the best ones. Brooks believed that most all-star teams failed because they relied too heavily on individual talent, not team chemistry. As we know, he was right. By combining the entire team's talents, the U.S. was able to beat the Russians in the semifinal round and go on to beat Finland to win the gold medal. As for the dynamics of all-star teams, just look at the 2004 U.S. Olympic Basketball Team. It was made up of the 12 best professional players—individuals with special talents who never played together as a team. In the end, the U.S. team finished with only a bronze medal, behind Italy and Argentina, which won the silver and gold, respectively.

My point here is this: Great teams aren't created by assembling individual superstars. A team's success depends on how well the talented team members interact and work together. You don't want 10 team members with the exact same skills, or team members with skills that don't mesh. The same is true for portfolio correlation. Investors who spread their assets among the best investments, funds and managers mistakenly think their portfolio will automatically do well. Actually, their *team* will perform no better than the 2004 Olympic basketball team. You're assuming way too much risk if you spread your assets among several firms to manage diversification and risk. You're also assuming too much risk if your wealth advisor isn't verifying that your investments, funds and managers are working together to provide checks and balances with different market movements and without excessive overlaps and conflicts.

Your portfolio needs these checks and balances because different types of investments react differently in different situations. Your portfolio may include mutual funds, closed-end funds, unit investment trusts, real estate investment trusts, hedge funds, exchange-traded funds and qualified exchange funds. Each fund provides diversified holdings that in some cases may clash with each other or result in portfolio redundancies. For example, hedge funds use any number of investment strategies, including stocks, bonds, commodities, currencies and return-enhancing tools such as leverage, derivatives and arbitrage. Real estate investment trusts invest in shopping malls, office towers, apartment buildings and healthcare facilities—but generally offer lower market-to-price volatility than stocks. If you own both—as many affluent investors do—there is the risk that the holdings in these two funds may be working at cross-purposes or may clash with other investments held by your portfolio. Clearly, your wealth advisor must invest in such a way that investment overlap and conflicts are minimized.

What criteria should you and your wealth advisor use in the selection and retention of your portfolio's investments, funds and managers? Each must be able to stand alone as being excellent, and each also must correlate or interrelate appropriately with the other investments, funds and managers in your portfolio. This is vital for the protection of your wealth. Managing the whole is as important as managing each part—and managing the whole is almost impossible if you spread your assets out among different firms. Here again is the argument for one wealth manager who ensures that your portfolio is well allocated, regularly rebalanced and reallocated, and made up of a group of investments that work well together.

When to Consider Two Portfolios

In almost all situations, I advise treating your assets as one large portfolio, with one trusted wealth advisor to oversee your entire investment landscape. But if your invested assets are worth $5 million to $10 million or more, you may want to consider having your wealth advisor split your portfolio in two—one to fund your capital lifetime needs and another for your *wealth surplus*.

Your *capital lifetime needs* portfolio is set up to support you during your retirement and will be managed actively, rebalanced when the market drives it out of balance, and reallocated when your current situation, future, feelings and family dynamics change. When you're near retirement, you may need to reallocate the portfolio based on these factors.

For your *wealth surplus* portfolio, you will take a more strategic approach to managing its asset allocation. Your wealth surplus portfolio is for the super-long term and designed to preserve wealth for future generations and any charitable inclinations you may have. Here you'll rebalance when the market distorts your allocation, but you won't reallocate as often. That's because this portfolio has more time to weather extended market declines. So, these two portfolios' asset allocations will look completely different even though they belong to the same person. Many families find that having these two portfolios allows them to more efficiently manage their total net worth over specific time periods and for different purposes.

CHECKLIST

1. Hire a trusted wealth advisor to help you structure an appropriate asset allocation for your entire investment portfolio.

2. Be sure the advisor's firm has an *open architecture*, which allows the advisor to buy any investment, fund or manager.

3. Avoid spreading assets among multiple firms to manage diversification and risk. This strategy actually increases risk.

4. Work with your wealth advisor to create an appropriate asset allocation that takes into consideration your current situation, your future needs, your feelings and your family dynamics.

5. Work with your wealth advisor to create a disciplined rebalancing process—for example, when assets rise or fall 10% above or below your original allocations.

6. Rebalance when your portfolio changes; reallocate when your current situation, future feelings or family dynamics change.

7. Insist that your wealth advisor selects investments, funds and managers that are excellent on their own and correlate and interrelate approximately with the other investments, funds and managers in your portfolio. Be sure your advisor reviews your portfolio for excessive overlap conflicts and lack of appropriate checks and balances.

8. Create two portfolios if your invested assets are greater than $5 to $10 million. Use one to fund your lifetime needs and allocate assets accordingly. Allocate the second portfolio for longer-term needs—inheritance of younger generations.

2

Insuring for Wealth Protection

Tragically, too many people I meet view life insurance, disability insurance, long-term-care insurance and personal liability insurance as a waste of money. Or they buy too little coverage because they misjudge their true needs. This is tragic because without adequate financial protection against life's random events, you, your family and your wealth are exposed to enormous risk.

Yes, the odds are that you will live a long, healthy and productive life. Most people do. But what if life doesn't turn out exactly as planned? What if you do everything right but are still saddled with a health problem, become the victim of an accident or are the target of a personal-injury lawsuit? Bad things happen to good people all the time, and the bad things that happen don't even have to be your fault.

The purpose of insurance is to safeguard against life's *what ifs*, and to ensure that your family won't suffer unnecessary financial hardship if those *what ifs* become *uh ohs*.

In my travels, I have found that most people who put off buying insurance do so because they don't think they will ever need the benefits. Others skip insurance because they don't understand how a policy works. Or they feel the whole process is too much of a hassle. Still others delay buying coverage because the entire subject is a downer and makes them feel badly about their future. Or they secretly worry that the mere act of thinking about coverage will somehow attract misfortune.

No one can predict or control the ups and downs we will experience in life. And I know of no study that shows a correlation between looking at an insurance policy and bad luck. Plain and simple, insurance coverage guarantees that your family and the wealth you've accumulated will not suffer should you be disabled, sued, remain ill for a long period of time or even die.

In this chapter, I will explain how life, disability, long-term-care and liability insurance can protect your wealth.

LIFE INSURANCE

I know firsthand what can happen when you do not have adequate life insurance. In 1962, after an chartered passenger jet crashed in Paris and killed more than 100 people from Atlanta, I was hired by a local bank to help settle their descendents' estates. Most were relatively young and wealthy, and had assumed that their large estates would be sufficient to care for their spouses in the event of death. What they never had imagined was that an accident could take the lives of both spouses, leaving their heirs with large estates that faced staggering estate taxes. In many cases, those estates did not have liquid assets to pay these estate taxes and were forced to sell other assets at discounted prices. Many of those who died that day were also the owners of businesses that suddenly didn't have a CEO or president or founder to continue making critical company decisions. As a result, in the years that followed, businesses struggled to regain their footing without sufficient resources to tide them over until new leaders could be recruited and trained.

Today, about half of all American families do not have life insurance. Of those who do have life insurance, a large percentage do not have enough coverage to enable family members to continue funding their current lifestyle or provide liquid assets to pay taxes at the death of the person bringing in the large annual income.

Before I discuss the different ways to use life insurance to protect your wealth, let's first simply define the two different types of policies available to you:

- **Cash value life insurance**—provides coverage until the end of life as well as a tax-favored savings account. How does this work? Each year, when you mail in your premium, a part is used to pay for life insurance while the remaining part is saved or invested, depending on the policy. The cash you put in the savings account is allowed to grow tax-free until you withdraw assets or cash in the policy. If the policy is in force when you die, the proceeds go to your beneficiary free of any federal income tax. Different types of cash-value policies include whole life, universal life, variable life and variable universal life.

• **Term life insurance**—provides only life insurance and for a specific number of years. While the annual premium for a term policy is significantly lower than the premium for a cash-value policy offering the same coverage, a term policy should be considered only if you need coverage for specific needs that end after a set period of time. Term insurance becomes prohibitively expensive in time if the insured individual lives to an old age. There are two types of term policies—level term and annual renewable term.

Generally, there are five reasons why people need life insurance. Let's look at each one:

1. To replace your income. When you have young children, it's important to have a pool of funds available for them if you die that can generate income to supplement their living expenses. Such expenses include not only basic care but also the cost of education, including college and graduate school.

As a result, you must be sure you have an appropriate level of life insurance coverage. Back in 1962, I saw many cases where the orphaned children of those who died in that Air France crash had to live with aunts and uncles. The situations that turned out best for the children were those where guardians had sufficient funds to not only pay the estate taxes of deceased parents but also cover the cost of raising the children. How much life insurance is appropriate? Your wealth advisor can help you assess your needs and find a policy that meets those needs.

2. To provide cash to pay estate taxes. If your estate is significant in size and you expect federal or state estate taxes will be owed, you have a choice: You can do nothing now and let your estate pay the tax when you die, or you can take out life insurance now to help your estate pay the tax bill. If you say you want to have your estate cover the estate tax, you've basically decided to let your children and descendents pay them. When I tell some clients this, they say, "Good, let my children pay the estate taxes. I don't want to make them wealthy anyway. I want them to work for their wealth, just as I did." My answer is, "Fine, let's not worry about the children for now. Let's talk about your wealth. You worked hard to create your wealth, didn't you?"

"I certainly have," they say.

Then I say, "If you worked so hard to create your wealth, why wouldn't you work just as hard to protect your wealth? What if when you die, up to 50% of what you stayed awake nights worrying about all those years has to go to the IRS as an unrestricted gift?"

Most people look at me puzzled. Why would the payment be considered an unrestricted gift, they ask.

Because if you don't have to hand over money and you do anyway, I call that a gift—you're getting nothing in return. The gift is unrestricted because the executor of your will can't designate how your taxes can be used. Then I tell clients that they don't have to let 50% of what they worked so hard to accumulate go to the IRS. How? By having your wealth advisor provide information on the coverage needed and costs of insurance to provide liquid funds to be used for estate taxes. This policy can be purchased using an irrevocable life insurance trust.

An irrevocable trust is nonreversible. That means once you set it up and place assets inside, you cannot remove them. When you place a life insurance policy inside the trust, the death benefit on that policy passes directly to the trust when you die, thereby avoiding your taxable estate and escaping the estate tax. Then your estate can tap into the death benefit to meet any estate tax obligations rather than selling your estate's assets, which may be perfectly invested or not easy to cash out. Not only will the policy's death benefit provide liquidity to pay estate taxes, leaving your other assets intact, but beneficiaries also will be able to invest whatever is left. Or you can set parameters on how remaining trust assets can be used.

If your only goal with an insurance policy is to provide your estate with cash to pay taxes on you and your spouse's combined estate, consider taking out a second-to-die policy for the life insurance trust. Unlike a traditional life insurance policy on one life, a second-to-die policy's death benefit isn't paid until the second insured person—usually the surviving spouse—dies. This policy is normally purchased when estate taxes will be sizable.

Why bother taking out such a policy? As you probably know, federal tax law allows for a *marital deduction*, which lets one spouse leave unlimited assets to his or her spouse tax-free. However, when those assets are inherited and combined, the surviving spouse's total estate is likely to be much larger. The result is that the surviving spouse's estate will be more likely to face estate taxes upon death. What if the federal estate tax is repealed? My answer is what if it isn't—or it is repealed and then reinstated? And don't forget that the state in which you live will almost certainly boost its estate tax threshold and rates to make up the shortfall as the federal threshold and rates phase out or disappear entirely.

The death benefit from a second-to-die life insurance policy inside a life insurance trust can help your estate pay any estate taxes without having to tap into the illiquid estate itself. Consult your wealth advisor and estate attorney to find out whether such a policy is ideal for your family's needs.

3. To fund a buy-sell agreement. When the owner of a company dies suddenly, that person's spouse and children often must scramble to find a buyer if they cannot step in and run the business. Each day that passes without the business having leadership increases the odds of that company's failure. With the clock ticking, heirs often are at a terrible disadvantage: Not only may they lack the knowledge to properly manage the business, they also may find they're being offered only low bids because potential buyers know they are desperate to sell.

A *buy-sell* agreement eases this pressure. *Buy-sell* agreements are also used when business partners or employees have an agreement to buy the business at the death of a partner or owner. The agreement establishes in advance a buyer and a predetermined price or price formula for the business in the event of the owner's death. But in some cases the buyer named in the agreement may be in poor financial shape when the owner dies and may need time to sign a note to the estate or raise cash to make the purchase and take ownership.

A life insurance policy can provide the cash necessary to fund the purchase price as defined in the buy-sell agreement. Without a life-insurance-funded buy-sell agreement, estates may be forced to sell the business at a low price or struggle financially.

I know a financial planner in Kansas City who recently had a 46-year-old client. The client owned a lucrative manufacturing business worth about $8 million, and was married with a 5-year-old son. Although this business owner's wealth advisor urged him to set up a life-insurance-funded buy-sell agreement, the owner responded, "I'm in great health. I don't really have to worry about that now."

But within the year, the owner was killed in an auto accident outside of Kansas City. His wife was the executrix of his estate and, with the help of the attorney for the estate, realized she couldn't manage the business and had to sell it. But she had trouble finding a buyer, and the business suffered. Finally, she found a company in California that was willing to buy her husband's business. But the company didn't have enough cash and couldn't borrow from the bank, so she accepted a note for the full amount due. She didn't have much choice.

A year after the company took possession of her husband's business, no payments had been made on the note. Soon the spouse received word that the acquiring company was bankrupt and that she was considered an unsecured creditor. As a result, she got nothing out of the business, which collapsed with the purchasing company's bankruptcy.

What makes this story particularly sad is that there was no reason for the surviving spouse to wind up losing $8 million. There was simply a lack of advanced planning. If her husband had set up a life-insurance-funded buy-sell agreement, his wife would not have had to sell to an illiquid buyer. A buyer already would have been identified, and the widow would have been able to prudently sell the business.

A common mistake business owners make when funding a buy-sell agreement with a life insurance policy is taking out too little coverage, based on a flawed valuation of their business. Many buy-sell agreements include a buy-out price, and business owners typically purchase life insurance to fund the buyout. However, if the business value is appraised low and the IRS determines the business is worth substantially more than the price in the buy-sell agreement, estate taxes will be owed. In some cases, this tax bill will leave little or no money from the life insurance proceeds for the surviving spouse to live on Therefore, it is important to have the business carefully appraised when the buy-sell agreement is created and enough life insurance to fund the fair market value of the business. The amount of insurance needed to fund the buy-sell agreement should be periodically reviewed to be sure it is sufficient to provide needed liquidity.

Discuss with your wealth advisor the best way to assure that your business can be sold after your death. Also, be sure to review your company's valuation and the life insurance policy regularly. Over time, the value of your business can increase significantly, which means your buy-sell agreement and insurance coverage should be adjusted upward.

4. To protect the value of a key business executive. If you own a company and you (and other executives) are the major decision-makers in the business, your company will likely need a cash infusion if you or those other executives died suddenly. The company will need the cash to meet its financial obligations while new top executives are recruited and trained, which in some cases can take months or years.

The solution is *key person* life insurance. Your company is the owner of the life insurance policy, pays the premiums and is the beneficiary upon your death or the death of key employees. The death benefits are received tax-free.

In addition to keeping your company solvent, the death benefit also can help replace profits the company could have earned had the key person lived, improving the company's balance sheet and assuring creditors and vendors that the business is financially sound.

How much is a key employee worth? You will have to work with your wealth advisor and attorney to project anticipated profit losses, replacement costs and a compensation-multiple formula.

5. To fund deferred compensation. Whenever you have a life insurance policy that is insuring a temporary death need, any cash value that has been built up in the policy can be used to supplement the retirement income of the insured. For example, an executive with key-person insurance who does not die before retirement no longer needs the death benefit. In such cases the cash value, if properly structured by having the insured pay some of the premium, can be distributed income-tax-free to the insured at retirement.

Reviewing a Life Insurance Policy

If you are fully insured, consider having a policy review done to determine whether you can obtain an additional death benefit for the same premium or the same death benefit at a lower premium. You do this using a *1035 exchange*—an IRS rule that lets you exchange the cash value from one insurance policy with another without sustaining capital gains or losses, provided the second policy is of greater value.

People always ask me whether it's truly possible to find insurance policies with terms that are more favorable than policies taken out when they were years younger. The answer is yes. Why? As more people live longer, the mortality tables used by insurance companies show that people are living longer. In other words, life insurance premiums can be less expensive today than when your policies were purchased. With a 1035 exchange, you can use the cash value of present policies to purchase new policies; your future premiums may be lower, and death benefits should be higher.

Your wealth advisor can help you find new policies through a policy review process.

Surrendering a Life Insurance Policy

If you no longer need a life insurance policy, for a number of reasons, and you are older than 65, don't assume that terminating your policy and withdrawing the cash value, if any, is the best move.

In fact, you may be able to receive two to three times your policy's cash value through a *life settlement*. A life settlement lets you sell your policy to a third party for a sum that's considerably higher than your cash value. How is this possible? There are companies that act as brokers to identify potential investors that purchase many life insurance policies. The new owner then would collect the proceeds upon the insured's passing. But don't get bogged down here. All that matters to you is that you can receive more than your cash value when giving up a policy, and your wealth advisor can help you find the companies that broker such settlements. Consider a life settlement when you are age 65 or older and:

- You no longer want or need the policy
- You need income to pay medical bills

- You can no longer afford the premium
- You're thinking about letting the policy lapse
- Your estate plans have changed
- You are considering purchasing a new policy

Most types of life insurance policies qualify for a life settlement, including universal life, whole life and convertible term life (which is a term life policy that allows you to convert it to a cash value policy). You'll need to consult your wealth advisor and accountant about any specific tax liability resulting from insurance settlement transactions.

DISABILITY INSURANCE

If one day you cannot work because of a health problem or a disability, your family may be able to make ends meet for as long as your company's short-term disability coverage lasts. Or until you recover and return to work. But what if your ailment or disability lasts for years? Or you cannot perform the job you were trained to do?

While the odds of this type of health crisis hitting you and your household seem relatively low, studies show that a third of all Americans between the ages 35 and 65 will be disabled for more than 90 days, and one in seven workers will be disabled for more than five years. Should such an event happen to you, your wealth would be seriously threatened.

Many people forget how critical their salary income is to paying household bills and maintaining cash flow. If your salary income were to be severely cut back or to stop, the impact would be felt almost immediately. Your family would have no alternative but to start tapping into the income produced by your wealth, or even to draw down the principal, to sustain your household's standard of living.

Most people say they don't need to purchase disability insurance because their company already provides it. I would urge you to have your company policy reviewed by your wealth advisor. Many employer policies pay 50% to 60% of your salary in the event of long-term disability lasting 26 weeks. But that amount won't likely provide nearly the income your family will require if you cannot work for an extended period of time. As a result, consider purchasing a supplemental disability policy on your own to cover the extra 20% to 30% of your income. Insurers typically won't insure up to 100% of your gross salary, because such coverage would remove your incentive to return to work. The two most important aspects of a disability policy are:

- **Who pays the premium?** If your company pays, any actual benefits are fully taxable. If you pay the premium, the benefits are tax-exempt. Therefore, if the company pays, you need more coverage.

- **What's the policy's definition of *disability*?** Consider an *own-occupation* policy, which provides a benefit if you cannot do the job you had before your disability even if you are physically able to perform another job.

Disability policies vary from insurer to insurer, and choosing one based solely on a low premium can be a mistake. Your wealth advisor can help assess your disability insurance needs and find the best policies available to you.

LONG-TERM-CARE INSURANCE

There is still quite a bit of debate over the value of long-term-care insurance. There are experts on both sides who have valid points as to why this type of insurance is a good or bad idea.

Personally, I'm in favor of long-term-care insurance, and here's why: You probably will spend a large portion of your life working hard to create wealth, but may wind up living incapacitated longer than you imagined or expected. We know from studies that people today not only are healthier than previous generations, but also that improved healthcare, treatments and medications are doing a better job of preventing illness and fighting disease. This means that when you become seriously ill, there is a greater chance of being ill or incapacitated for longer periods of time.

If you need care during a long period of illness, the expense of at-home nursing or a room in a private nursing facility can cost tens of thousands of dollars a month. Remember, Medicaid and your employer's health insurance plan will not cover long-term-care costs, and Medicare just covers skilled nursing care and only for a limited time period.

In most cases, the cost of long-term care will have to come out of your family's pocket, which means your wealth is at risk. A long-term-care policy can minimize the amount your family has to pay out of pocket, which in turn protects the wealth you created from being drained for your care.

When you and your wealth advisor shop for long-term-care policies, be sure to ask:

- **When are benefits paid?** Long-term-care policies typically kick in when you cannot perform a certain number of activities of daily living, including bathing and dressing, and need at-home or facility care.

- **What types of facilities and care are covered?**

- **What type of care is covered?** A good policy will cover all levels of care—including custodial or personal care.

- **Is a *waiver of premium* included?** This provision lets you stop paying premiums when you are receiving benefits.

- **How long do you have to be in a nursing home**—before premiums are waived? From 60 to 90 days is standard.

- **Is the policy *guaranteed renewable*?** This means the insurer guarantees you the chance to renew your policy.

At what age should you start to look at long-term care? If you listen to the pundits, many say, "Don't bother taking out a policy until age 59. Oh really? I was talking to a person recently who was 44 years old. He said every person in his family had died of either a heart attack or cancer. He also said that the chances are he would have to undergo similar treatments. As a result, he bought a long-term-care policy.

The younger you are when you take out the policy, the lower the policy premium will be. A good rule of thumb is to look into a policy when you're approaching your mid-50s. Some people may want to begin looking at policies at an earlier age. Remember, Christopher Reeve was only 42 years old when he was permanently injured in a horse accident in 1995, and needed care until 2004, when he passed away. The fact is you never know.

PERSONAL LIABILITY INSURANCE

People today are quick to hire a lawyer to settle their differences or seek financial satisfaction if they feel they've been injured in some way. It's a fact of life. We live in litigious times, and those lawsuits can come with steep financial settlements that can eat into your wealth.

Consider this: Between 1984 and 2000, the chief reason most people fell off the Forbes 400 Richest People in America list, other than market fluctuations reducing the size of their wealth, had to do with legal issues.

I was speaking with someone recently from Texas who keeps a small dog behind a fence in his backyard. One day the dog broke out and chased a jogger running on the street. The jogger tripped and broke her collarbone and wrist. So she sued the owner for $250,000. In her lawsuit, she claimed that the dog's pursuit required her to increase her gait to a level not normally used in her athletic endeavors, leading to her fall and injury and suffering.

Suits like this occur every day—even when you take measures to protect people who interact with your family members and your property. If a friend of your child is injured on your property, if a neighbor drinks to excess at your house and hits someone driving home, if your teenage child punches another teen, or if someone using your pool is injured on your diving board—all of these aggrieved parties will have grounds for a personal injury lawsuit.

While most auto insurance policies provide some liability coverage, judgments stemming from injuries typically exceed policy limits, especially if there is a critical injury or loss of life. You're an even bigger target for liability lawsuits if you have a high level of net worth or are a prominent member of your community, because people who sue assume you'd rather settle or have deep pockets.

As a result, you should consider a *personal excess liability policy*—also known as an *umbrella liability policy*—which offers you additional coverage in $1 million increments over and above your basic homeowner or auto coverage. Ask your wealth advisor to review your umbrella liability policy, the terms of the coverage and how much coverage is sufficient given your wealth and the risks to your wealth if you're sued and a judgment is awarded.

1. See if you have sufficient life insurance coverage.

2. Consider a life insurance trust if estate taxes will be owed.

3. If your life insurance policy is three years old, have it reviewed.

4. Consider a 1035 exchange if you find a better life insurance policy.

5. If you plan to surrender a life insurance policy, consider a *life settlement.*

6. If you own a business, consider a life-insurance-funded buy-sell agreement to protect the value for heirs. Also consider *key person* life insurance.

7. See if your company's disability insurance policy is sufficient.

8. Consider buying additional disability insurance coverage—but verify the definition of *disability.*

9. Consider buying long-term-care insurance coverage.

10. Consider boosting your level of liability insurance protection.

3

BORROWING TO CREATE AND PROTECT WEALTH

Debt is an emotional issue for many people. Just the thought of borrowing money and owing interest payments over long periods of time can make some people feel financially trapped and vulnerable. Others equate debt with poor money management skills and shame. Interestingly, I've found that many of the people with the greatest phobia of debt know relatives who borrowed too much and struggled too long and hard to make loan payments, a battle that led ultimately to financial hardships and family tensions.

If you are philosophically opposed to debt, I completely understand your concerns. Debt is indeed dangerous. Millions of people each year wind up in financial trouble because they overestimate their ability to fund both household expenses and regular debt payments. They never anticipated that their income—high when they borrowed money—might dip during the loan-payment period, forcing them to scramble to pay the bills. Many may wind up unable to sleep nights, worrying that they may need to borrow more just to meet existing loan payments.

But debt itself is not evil. Taking out loans to temporarily ease financial stress, own a necessity such as a car, or buy equity positions or real property today that will be worth more tomorrow can actually create wealth. For example, if you put down 10% to buy a $2 million rental property, you've borrowed funds to buy a property costing 10 times your cash investment. The property not only will reward you if its value climbs over time, but also will generate rental income that you can use to offset costs and pay bills. This is called *leverage*—the use of borrowed money to make more money.

As you can see, if you use debt wisely, you can generate wealth as well as protect and preserve the wealth you've already accumulated. But before you borrow, you must always carefully select the right loan for your needs, find the lender with the best terms and rates and evaluate your capacity to meet debt payments. That's why I urge you to involve your wealth advisor and accountant in all decisions related to borrowing money.

In this chapter, I will tell you what you need to know before you borrow, how to size up a loan, when to borrow and which loans to use.

Before You Borrow

Whenever borrowing money seems to make sense for your financial needs, keep these three considerations in mind before going forward:

1. **The loan's cost.** You and your wealth advisor need to look at the cost of a loan (the interest rate) compared with inflation—the annual increase in the price of goods and services. If you can borrow money at a low interest rate and use the money to buy something you need today that will become more expensive in the future, chances are a loan makes sense. In effect, you will be paying for an asset over time using cheaper dollars. To simplify, image you could take out a loan to buy four year's worth of gasoline at the current price per gallon. If gas prices rise over the next four years, you'll still be filling up at today's pump price. In other words, you've borrowed money at a low interest rate to buy an asset and are paying less for it over the long run. That's why interest rates and the annual inflation rate are crucial when determining whether to take out a loan. If inflation is on the rise, interest rates typically will rise as the Federal Reserve attempts to slow rapid economic growth. As a result, borrowing before rates increase is beneficial.

2. **The loan's terms.** While the cost to borrow money—the interest rate—is always important, so are a deal's terms. For example, if a loan does not require you to pledge personal assets

as collateral, the asset protection you gain may be worth more than a slight reduction in the loan's interest rate.

3. **The loan's impact on your finances.** How the loan fits in with your overall portfolio and wealth-accumulation plan is essential. Before you borrow, you and your wealth advisor need to study your balance sheet to determine your total debt and see how the loan you're considering will affect your ability to manage your other liabilities. Your wealth advisor not only can help you determine whether you can afford to borrow the amount you need, but also whether you are using the right lender. People who view borrowing as an isolated financial event and do not consider debt to be part of their cash flow or wealth-creation always astonish me.

SIZING UP A LOAN

People borrow money for many different reasons. For some, a loan will be used for personal purposes—to buy a car, a second home or artwork, for example. For others, the loan will be used for business purposes—to ease a cash crunch or take advantage of an opportunity. Once you have decided to borrow money, there are seven important questions to ask:

1. **What type of loan do you need?** There are many different types of loans. Determining which one is right for you depends on when your interest payments and principal are due. For example, most home-equity lines of credit have a set term, such as 10 years. No matter how much you draw on your credit line, the entire balance will need to be paid off or refinanced when that time period elapses. A home-equity credit line is an example of a *time loan*, which has a specific payoff period. By contrast, a *demand loan* can be called for payment by the lender at any time. A *balloon loan* lets you make level monthly payments, with the loan's balance due in a lump sum at the end of a specific period. A *bridge loan* allows repayment to be tied to a specific event in the near term, such as the sale of a property or receipt of business receivables. As you can see, there are many

different types of loans. You and your wealth advisor need to discuss which loan offers the best fit for your need.

2. **What's the loan's rate and terms?** As you evaluate different types of loans, you and your wealth advisor will need to establish each loan's true interest rate. Too many people today are fooled by the loan's introductory or *teaser* rate used prominently in advertisements. An introductory rate typically is rock bottom but in place only for an initial period—such as six months or a year—after which a higher annual percentage rate (APR) kicks in for the loan's duration. The APR on the loan you're considering should be consistent with the going rate on similar types of loans made by institutions with similar levels of credit risk.

In addition to rates, all loans come with terms set by the lender. If you borrow from a friend or relative, the terms of the loan may simply require you to communicate in writing annually with the person who loaned you the money. But if you borrow from an institution, the lender may require you to obtain title to the property you're buying, insure it, invest enough of your own money to have a committed interest, and make loan payments on time. Other terms may include requiring you to hold a sufficient equity position in the property, restricting dividend payouts and reserving cash flow from operations and sale of assets. Your wealth advisor can help you determine if a loan's rate and terms are ideal for you.

3. **What are the lender's policies?** Every lender has a unique set of policies that must be carefully scrutinized before you sign documents. Most of these policies are in place to ensure in advance that you can repay the loan on time. One policy may require you to have a specific *loan-to-value* ratio (LTV), which ensures that you have enough of your own money invested in the deal so you won't abandon the asset to avoid repayment. For example, if a lender's LTV ratio is 80%, it will lend you up to 80% of an asset's value, provided you have at least 20% of your own money invested. Generally, the higher a bank's

LTV—meaning the less it requires you to invest in the asset— the more stringent its borrowing terms.

Another mortgage-lender policy is the *housing expense ratio* (HER), which is calculated by adding up your monthly loan principal and interest payments, real estate taxes and homeowner's insurance, and dividing the sum by your gross monthly income. Banks typically accept an HER of 28% or less.

You also should be aware of an institution's *total obligations ratio* (TOR), which is calculated by dividing your total monthly expenses (not just the payments related to the property you're buying) by your gross monthly income. Each institution accepts a different ratio.

The closer the relationship you or your wealth advisor has with a bank, the more likely the bank will adjust its policies as much as possible in your favor. That's because the bank is more likely to be comfortable with you and trust you based on your or your wealth advisor's past dealings with the institution. In fact, just expressing an interest in hearing more about how to invest securities through the bank may improve the lender's policies on your loan. Several banks already have stated publicly that if they added no new clients but converted each of their existing loan customers into investment clients, they would become the largest investment firm in the U.S.

4. **What's your cash flow?** Before borrowing money, you need to know whether you will have sufficient cash available each month to meet your loan payments and household expenses. Your wealth advisor can help you create a *source and use of funds* list to see if you can afford the loan you're seeking. This exercise should include the creation of a cash-flow statement (income, expenses and taxes) for last year and the current year as well as a projection for the years in which you're borrowing the money.

5. **What's your net worth?** Many people overestimate their net worth because they do not take all of their liabilities into consideration. Liabilities include mortgages, credit card balances,

margin debt and any other balances due to lenders. Your wealth advisor can help you create a net-worth statement—a snapshot of your financial health at a particular date in time. A net-worth statement summarizes what you own (your assets) and what you owe (your liabilities or debts). To calculate your net worth, you simply subtract your total liabilities from your total assets. Be sure to use the fair market value for all assets at the time you make this calculation.

The result will tell you and your wealth advisor how additional debt will affect your wealth, and whether you can afford the liability. The rule of thumb is that your assets should be able to cover your liabilities fully, which is a ratio of 1:1. Higher ratios (over 2:1) are more attractive to lenders. This is called your *leverage ratio* and is determined by dividing your total debt by your total assets. Your financial advisor can help you determine this ratio before you borrow and monitor your ratio after the money is loaned.

6. **What's your credit score?** Your credit score is a three-digit number that sums up your creditworthiness. Credit scores range from 300 to 850—the higher your score, the less risky you are to lenders. If your score is above the national median (about 720), you're considered an excellent credit risk and will likely qualify for a lender's most favorable rates and terms. By contrast, a score below 620 is a red flag for lenders.

The credit industry's most widely accepted measurement of creditworthiness is your FICO score. It is calculated by Fair Isaac Inc. using data reported by your creditors to the three major credit bureaus—Equifax, Experian and TransUnion. The fastest way to get your credit score and all three credit reports is to go to *www.MyFICO.com* and, for a fee, you will be able to receive all of this information online within minutes.

Before you apply for a loan, you and your wealth advisor should access your credit reports and credit score and clear up any mistakes that may be dragging your score down. Don't think your credit report contains mistakes? According to studies, 25% of all credit reports have errors. If your credit report is mistake-free but your credit score is low, you may want to delay your loan application so you can take steps to try and boost your score. Be sure your wealth advisor reviews all of these documents and that you check your report and score annually.

7. **Is the loan tax-efficient?** Before you borrow money, you and your wealth advisor should be sure the loan you've chosen is the most tax-efficient way to access the funds you need. For example, the interest payments on primary mortgages, home-equity lines of credit and margin loans are tax deductible when assets are borrowed for specific purposes.

WHEN TO BORROW

Now that you know the virtues of borrowing money and the types of questions you need to ask before applying for a loan, let's look at the different situations when borrowing is ideal:

Mortgage loans. Traditional mortgage loans are sought from banks and other financial institutions. In general, there are two types of home mortgages—a fixed-rate mortgage and an adjustable-rate mortgage. A fixed-rate mortgage lets you to lock in an interest rate for the duration of the loan—regardless of whether national mortgage rates rise or fall over time.

By contrast, an adjustable-rate mortgage (ARM) offers an interest rate that's *variable*—or tied to a market indicator such as the weekly average of one-year Treasury Bills. Most ARMs limit how often its interest rate changes to every six months or once a year.

There are many different types of ARMs. Most ARMs offer a fixed rate for a set period of months or years before switching to a variable rate for the duration of the loan. In most cases, an ARM's initial rate is lower than a traditional fixed-rate loan for the same time period to make the ARM more attractive and to offset the variable-rate risk that kicks in after the fixed-rate period elapses.

Which mortgage is right for you? That depends on many factors, including how long you plan to own the property, how much you plan to put down, and how much you can afford each month in mortgage payments. In general, if you don't intend to own the property for more than five to seven years, an ARM may make more sense. That's because its initial fixed rate is lower than a comparable fixed-rate loan and you're likely to sell the property before the higher variable rate kicks in. However, if you plan to own the property for 10 years or longer, a fixed-rate mortgage probably makes more sense.

Another important factor is the anticipated direction of interest rates. If interest rates are low when you plan to borrow but are expected to rise, a 15- or 30-year fixed-rate loan is probably more ideal than an ARM. You'll be able to lock in a low rate for the full length of the loan, regardless of how high interest rates or mortgage rates climb in the future. Your wealth advisor can help you determine which mortgage is best for you.

Some mortgages contain hidden risks. For example, *interest-only* mortgages let you pay just the interest for a period of years before jumping significantly when the principal is added to the bill. *Option ARMs* give you the choice of making payments that do not cover the interest, which will cause your mortgage balance to balloon over time. And *piggyback loans* let you take out a loan to help meet the required mortgage down payment, but you may wind up overwhelmed with debt. Consulting your wealth advisor to determine the benefits and drawbacks of any mortgage is essential—even if advertisements for the mortgage or the marketing pitch from the lender makes the loan sound sweet.

When should you consider refinancing a mortgage? When the market rate available from lenders in your region is a point or two below the one on your current loan. But how you refinance requires careful analysis by your wealth advisor. For example, refinancing a 30-year mortgage at a lower interest rate can reduce your monthly loan payments and free up cash. But if you refinance instead to a mortgage with a shorter time period, you could pay off the loan sooner—and save significantly in interest payments. Here's how it works: Assume 10 years have passed since you took out a 30-year mortgage and that current rates are now one to two percentage points below your rate. If you refinance your 30-year loan to a 15-year mortgage, you could owe about the same amount each month in mortgage payments but you would pay off the loan five years sooner, avoiding tens of thousands of dollars in interest payments. But before you choose this option, consult your wealth advisor. Interest payments on a mortgage are tax deductible, so you will need to figure out whether the deduction or the savings is more advantageous. How close you are to retirement and whether you will be able to afford loan payments once you stop working full time also will need to be considered by your wealth advisor.

Refinancing an ARM to a fixed-rate mortgage can also be a smart strategy if interest rates decline sufficiently. Just be aware that refinancing restarts the clock. For example, refinancing an ARM with 10 years left to a 30-year, fixed-rate mortgage may not make financial sense given the term of the new 30-year loan—even if your monthly payments are lower.

Also beware of paying off your mortgage early. Many people I talk to do this with the best of intentions. They make extra payments each month or send in lump sums. You first need to determine if making accelerated mortgage payments each year makes financial sense. Early mortgage payments must be measured against the tax deduction you are receiving on the interest payment, your planned year of retirement and other factors. Your wealth advisor and accountant can help you here.

If your home has appreciated significantly in value, you may want to refinance your home-equity line of credit. As real estate rises in value, so does the amount institutions are willing to lend you based on your home-equity credit line. While you do not have to borrow a dime from this credit line, I think it's a good idea to have as much as possible available should you need it. Again, the rate on a home-equity credit line may be among the lowest in the lending marketplace, and interest payments in some cases are tax-deductible. Your wealth advisor can help you determine if refinancing makes sense, and can help you find a lender with the best rates and terms.

Bridge loans. Not all loans are needed for long periods of time. In some cases you may need to borrow a lump sum for just 30 to 90 days—the gap in time between the purchase of a new property and the sale of an old one. Or you may run a business and need cash until the company's value rises, but don't want to give up control of the business to investors. In both situations, you would seek a *bridge loan*.

A bridge loan bridges the gap between your need for cash today and the closing of a deal that will yield cash in the near future. This loan is similar to when you were a kid and needed a few extra bucks from your parents until allowance day. Banks and other financial institutions make bridge loans, but you also can turn to firms that specialize in bridge loans for businesses that need a temporary cash infusion. For example, if you run a business, you may be able to find a firm that's willing to pay 50% to 70% of your bills in exchange for 100% of the value of your invoices plus a fee or charge for the loan.

Before applying for a bridge loan, discuss your options with your wealth advisor and be sure you understand the risks as well as the loan's rates and terms.

Debt consolidation. Many of the people I meet who are carrying high levels of credit card debt tell me how difficult it is to pay down the balances, especially as their everyday expenses and interest rate charges on the debt mount.

Sadly, owing tens of thousands of dollars in credit card debt with high interest rates means you cannot invest all of those monthly card payments in your portfolio to further expand your wealth. As a result, your wealth may not grow as fast as it would have if you did not have hose credit card payments. Credit card balances can even threaten your wealth if you must use some of your principal investment to pay down part or all of what you owe. What's more, most credit card debt is what I call bad debt—money borrowed at high rates of interest to buy things that don't appreciate in value over time. Listen, there's nothing wrong with buying things that give you joy—such as family vacations, nice clothing and the latest electronics. Problems arise when luxury purchases become compulsions.

When you have an especially high credit card balance, your first goal should be to consolidate the debt with a loan that offers the lowest possible interest rate. In other words, it's more beneficial to use a loan that charges 4.5% interest to pay off balances on credit cards charging 12% or more.

One of the best loans for such a purpose is a home-equity credit line, which likely will have the lowest rates of interest available to you and the greatest flexibility. Just be sure to set up an aggressive schedule to pay down your credit line loan and avoid adding more debt to the cards you just paid off. Another way to reduce your credit card load is to pay off or reduce the balances using investment assets that no longer suit your portfolio's allocation. Just be sure you fully understand the tax implications of any trade.

Your wealth advisor can evaluate your credit card debt and help you develop strategic ways to reduce your balance while instituting a budget you can live with until the debt has been considerably reduced or erased.

Auto loans. Generally, there are three ways to pay for a car—you can pay cash, borrow the money or lease the vehicle. This decision is often made after reviewing a range of personal and financial considerations.

If you plan to borrow the cash needed for the purchase, many dealers offer ultra-low financing if your credit score is high and you are an excellent credit risk. Otherwise, you may not qualify for the best rate. A credit union typically offers car loans with attractive rates—if your company sponsors a credit union. Banks offer comparatively low rates, too.

Or you can tap into your home-equity credit line. While you won't be able to deduct the interest payments on a car, the credit line will likely have a comparatively low interest rate. If you borrow from this account, be sure to make payments to yourself monthly so the loan is paid on schedule.

Margin loans. Brokers and other financial institutions using your securities as collateral offer this type of loan. You can borrow up to 50% of the market value of your securities, and the proceeds are typically used to buy additional securities. You are allowed to deduct the interest paid up to the income you receive each year from the investments purchased with the loan. However, you can't deduct interest on a margin loan if it's used to purchase tax-exempt investments, such as municipal bonds. Consult your wealth advisor and accountant.

Margin loans come with risks that should be discussed with your wealth advisor in advance of borrowing. For example, if the securities used as collateral fall in value, you may suddenly be asked by your broker or financial institution to come up with cash immediately to secure the lost value. If you cannot do this, the institution will *call* or claim your securities. Of course, borrowing on margin can be highly advantageous if the securities you purchase with the loan rise in value.

Life insurance loans. If you own a cash-value life insurance policy and have built up sufficient savings in the cash-value portion, you can borrow from your policy. There's no term on the loan. In fact, you never have to repay what you've borrowed. However, any loan outstanding at the time of death will be deducted from the death benefit paid to beneficiaries. And you do have to pay interest on the amount you borrow and repay. Your wealth advisor and insurance advisor can help you here.

Specialty loans. There are lenders that specialize in loans for buying works of art, jewelry and other high-priced collectibles. Other specialty lenders make loans for the purchase of planes, boats or recreational vehicles. The names of such lenders often are available through auction houses, boat shows and other organizations that represent the makers of these high-end products. Your wealth advisor can help find and vet these lenders.

Trust loans. Some families set up family limited partnerships (FLPs), limited liability companies (LLCs) and trusts to allow businesses and other major assets to pass to heirs free of estate tax. In some cases, that asset may be a home with significant value. But what if you need to borrow money to renovate that house? Because the property is in a trust, many banks may not be willing to loan you the money because your collateral (the home) is in an irrevocable trust and cannot be accessed by you.

In such cases, your wealth advisor will need to coordinate with your estate attorney and locate lenders who specialize in making loans to high-net-worth individuals or families with special situations, such as borrowing against real estate owned inside FLPs, LLCs and trusts. As a result, your wealth advisor needs to understand your estate planning objectives and how they correlate with your wealth planning objectives.

CHECKLIST

1. Discuss loan plans with your wealth advisor.

2. Request your credit score and credit reports. Fix all mistakes.

3. Create net worth and cash flow statements.

4. See how many times your assets can cover liabilities.

5. Evaluate how much you can afford in monthly loan payments.

6. Determine which type of loans to consider.

7. Review the rates, terms, policies and tax-efficiency of each loan.

8. Determine if refinancing existing loans is prudent.

9. If property values have increased, consider refinancing home-equity lines of credit.

10. Pay off credit card debt or consolidate with a low-interest loan.

4

DISTRIBUTING RETIREMENT ASSETS TAX-EFFICIENTLY

Over time, you will likely amass significant wealth in your company-sponsored retirement plan and Individual Retirement Account (IRA). In fact, your 401(k) plan and IRA may wind up being your largest assets—worth more combined than your primary residence.

Yet many people lose sight of the fact that these plans were created to provide tax-favorable ways to fund your retirement. Some people cash out their plans at age 59½ and start gifting to heirs. Others try to stretch their retirement plans by not withdrawing assets until age 70½ and then take minimum distributions so that the accounts have a greater chance of passing to heirs when they die. Both strategies have merits in some cases but aren't nearly as efficient as using the plans' income streams to fund your retirement and using taxable assets for gifting and estate-planning purposes.

Another mistake many people make is not fully disclosing all of their retirement plan assets to one wealth advisor. If you do not inform your wealth advisor of your retirement accounts and provide regular updates, you can't possibly have an integrated asset allocation between all of your different accounts. You also will likely have overconcentrations in multiple accounts and wind up with muddled asset allocations. Your wealth advisor should manage both your retirement plan assets and your taxable portfolio so you have one comprehensive plan.

In this chapter, I will tell you about some of the different types of retirement plans available, the relevant contribution and distribution rules associated with those plans, and offer tax-efficient strategies available during your lifetime and at death to gift, donate and preserve your wealth.

YOUR RETIREMENT PLANS

Many of the tax-favored retirement plans we enjoy today date back to the Employee Retirement Income Security Act (ERISA) of 1974, which essentially relaxed the guidelines for private pension plans. By the early 1970s, Congress had become worried about the increasing number of employees who, despite having worked years at a one company or at many companies, were unable to receive traditional pension benefits.

Back then, many employees were not able to meet the requirements to qualify for company pensions. Other employees were left high and dry when pension plans were terminated before companies had accumulated enough assets to pay out. And Social Security was simply not designed to cover all the expense of an individual's retirement.

To address these concerns and the future financial needs of retirees, Congress created two landmark savings accounts—the *qualified retirement plan* (QRP), which eased company vesting schedules and standards for administrating retirement plans, and the individual retirement account (IRA), which gave individuals who didn't participate in a company-sponsored plan a tax-favored way to save.

In 1981, the IRS allowed for the creation of the 401(k), while new legislation expanded ERISA's rules and enabled employees enrolled in a QRP to also own an IRA.

Today, the QRP and the IRA are among the most powerful ways to build and preserve wealth. Let's look at how each works before we explore the rules and wealth preservation strategies:

Qualified retirement plan (QRP). Companies that offer a QRP must make them available to all employees. By doing so, your contributions and those made by your employer qualify for special tax breaks, including pretax contributions and tax-deferred growth. There are two categories of QRPs—defined contribution plans and defined benefit plans. For the purposes of this chapter, the defined contribution plan I will focus on is the 401(k), which a majority of affluent individuals own.

Individual Retirement Account (IRA). Anyone who earns a specific level of employment income is eligible to open a traditional IRA and make contributions up to the annual limit. Like assets in a QRP, the assets in an IRA grow on a tax-deferred basis. In the years since the traditional IRA was created in 1974, other types of IRAs have emerged, each with different rules. Here are the major ones:

- **Rollover IRA**—is an IRA you set up to receive assets from another retirement plan or IRA. You typically set up a Rollover IRA when you leave a company and want to transfer in 401(k) assets. Transferring assets into a Rollover IRA gives you more investment choices than those typically offered in a QRP, while retaining the account's tax-deferred status.

- **Roth IRA**—is similar to the traditional IRA, with a few key exceptions: You aren't required to take distributions at any age, you continue to receive tax-deferred growth for as long as you wish, withdrawals are tax-free after a five-year waiting period and contributions can be made at any age. However, you can open a Roth IRA only if you do not exceed specific income levels.

- **Simplified Employee Pension Plan IRA (SEP)**—to qualify for SEP IRA, you must operate a business or be self-employed. A SEP IRA is similar in many ways to a traditional IRA, except that a SEP IRA lets you contribute much more each year. Contributions are not taxable, provided they do not exceed your contribution limits.

CONTRIBUTION RULES

Under the current tax law, if you participate in a 401(k) plan you can defer up to $15,000 of your salary in 2006. If you're age 50 or older, you can defer up to $20,000. After 2006, the maximum annual contribution will be indexed for inflation in $500 steps.

Contributions to a traditional IRA are limited to $4,000 in 2006 and 2007, rising to $5,000 in 2008 and beyond. If you're age 50 or older, you can contribute $5,000 to an IRA in 2006 and 2007, and $6,000 in 2008 and beyond.

Of course, the biggest attraction of a 401(k) plan and IRA is their favorable tax treatment. Contributions to a 401(k) are on a pretax basis—meaning contributions are made before income winds up in your paycheck, thereby lowering your taxable income.

In a 401(k) and an IRA, invested assets grow on a tax-deferred basis—meaning there are no capital gains to pay on trades or on income and dividends. When assets are withdrawn, you're taxed at your ordinary income tax rate.

Given that your tax hit occurs when assets are withdrawn, you need to plan your distributions carefully. That's why it's essential to be familiar with plan distribution rules.

DISTRIBUTION RULES

Your age is critical when considering withdrawing assets from a 401(k) or IRA. Let's look at the rules:

Before age 59½. You are allowed to withdraw assets from an IRA retirement accounts before age 59½—but in most cases you will face a 10% early-distribution penalty in addition to income tax owed. However, there are exceptions: You will escape owing the stiff 10% penalty before age 59½ if withdrawals are used for:

- Medical expenses that exceed 7.5% of your adjusted gross income.
- Bills if you're disabled.
- College education expenses
- The purchase of a first-time home (only up to $10,000).
- Health insurance premiums after 12 consecutive weeks of unemployment.
- Payment pursuant to an IRS levy.
- Payment pursuant to a Qualified Domestic Relations Order (QDRO).

You also will not owe a 10% penalty if you take installment distributions from retirement accounts before age 59½ based on your life expectancy. Under Section 72(t) of the tax code, you will owe income tax on the distributions, and you must continue this annual life-expectancy withdrawal schedule for at least five years—or until you turn 59½. In other words, you cannot withdraw assets one year and not take distributions in the four years that follow.

You also are allowed to withdraw assets from a 401(k) retirement account before age 59½ in hardship cases if you are unemployed. In such cases, you will escape owing the 10% penalty before age 59½ if withdrawals are used for:

- Medical expenses that exceed 7.5% of your adjusted gross income.

- Bills if you're disabled.

- Payment to you after separation from employment after age 55.

- Payment pursuant to an IRS levy.

- Payment pursuant to a Qualified Domestic Relations Order (QDRO).

As with all decisions related to withdrawals before age 59½, review your plans carefully with your wealth advisor and make sure you understand the impact of removing assets early from any tax-deferred account.

At age 59½. When you reach this age, you have a choice: You can leave your assets in the account and let them continue to grow, tax-deferred. Or you can withdraw some or all of the assets without paying the 10% penalty—though you will owe income tax on the withdrawn assets.

At age 70½. At this age you no longer have a choice. You must start taking annual distributions based on IRS life-expectancy tables by April 1 in the year after you turn age 70½.

However, there are two exceptions: First, if you are married to a spouse who is at least 10 years younger than you are, you can use your joint life expectancy to arrive at a lower minimum withdrawal level. Second—and this exception exists only with a 401(k)—withdrawals may be delayed until age

75 if you have not yet retired (except if you're a 5% owner in the company where you work).

Fail to withdraw the required minimum amount each year starting at age 70½ and you could owe a 50% penalty on the amount you were supposed to remove—in addition to income tax.

DISTRIBUTION OPPORTUNITIES

Clearly, the age when most affluent people can start making strategic moves with their tax-deferred retirement accounts is 59½. At this age, you have three general choices—you can cash out all of the assets in your account, delay withdrawing assets until age 70½ or use the savings to fund your retirement expenses. I believe that in most cases the third option—living off the savings—is most beneficial. First, let's look at each option:

1. Cashing out. Affluent individuals who choose to withdraw all of their 401(k) or IRA savings typically do so to start gifting assets to heirs or to charitable causes to reduce the size of their estate and fulfill philanthropic missions. If you and your wealth advisor decide that withdrawing a lump sum from retirement plans is desirable, there are tax-efficient ways to accomplish this goal:

- **When making charitable gifts.** Many individuals who cash out of a retirement plan to fund charitable causes typically make a big tax error. They donate a large sum at once and find they are unable to qualify for the most favorable charitable tax deduction. Under the current tax law, individuals can contribute only 50% of their adjusted gross income to public charities before the tax code limits the amount of their deduction for the year. Donations to semipublic charities have a 30% cut-off point.

  My recommendation is that instead of making a sizable lump-sum donation in a single year, you are better off dividing the sum and making gifts over several years to make the most of your deduction. Consult your wealth advisor on the most tax-efficient way to make charitable cash donations.

- **When transferring company stock.** Many companies allow senior executives to buy shares of company stock for their 401(k) plans. If your company provides such a program, you have a powerful opportunity available when you retire at age 59½ or later. Instead of cashing out your entire 401(k) (or transferring the assets into a Rollover IRA), you may be better off transferring your company stock into a taxable account.

  Here's why: Normally, whenever you cash out a tax-deferred account, you owe income tax (federal, state and possibly local) on the withdrawal—a tax hit that could be high if you're in a top tax bracket. But because company stock in a 401(k) is considered a *qualified security*, the IRS recognizes only what you paid for that stock. So, for example, you could own company stock that's currently worth $15 million but only owe income tax on the $1 million you paid for the shares over the years.

  Once you transfer the stock to your taxable account and decide to sell shares, you will owe only the long-term capital gains tax. If you decide not to sell shares and leave some or all of them in the taxable account, be sure to reevaluate with your wealth advisor whether the company stock still is appropriate for your portfolio and whether the size of your position exceeds your portfolio's desired allocation based on your long-term goals.

  Transferring company stock to a taxable account under this rule also provides you with other tax-favorable opportunities. For example, once the shares are in a taxable account, you could sell a portion of the stock and offset the capital gains tax owed by donating another portion of the stock to charity, thereby creating a tax deduction. Discuss the benefit of such a move with your wealth advisor.

- **When funding a family limited partnership.** Another tax-efficient way to cash out of retirement plans to gift the proceeds to heirs during your lifetime is to use the assets to purchase a family limited partnership (FLP). By doing so, you qualify for the same asset discount that families receive when they set up an FLP for estate planning or business succession purposes. Consult your wealth advisor to determine if this strategy is appropriate for you and consider the IRS rules that must be followed.

2. Delaying your withdrawals. Many wealthy individuals attempt to stretch the status of their tax-deferred retirement accounts as long as possible by not making withdrawals until age 70½. Then they extend the status even further by taking only the required minimum distribution each year. This strategy typically is used to preserve the sizable assets for inheriting heirs, who in turn hopefully will retain them in their own IRAs and further extend the tax-favored status. The theory here is that the assets will last longer because heirs will withdraw smaller mandatory amounts each year, based on longer life expectancies.

But there are big flaws with this line of thinking. If you've done your job correctly, inheriting heirs will also be in a high tax bracket, meaning that their withdrawals will likely face maximum income taxes. In addition, heirs may say they intend to stretch the tax-favored status of an inherited 401(k) or IRA—but the reality is they will more likely cash out the assets, pay the stiff income tax bill, and still wind up with a tidy net sum to pay off credit card debt or make luxury purchases.

Lastly, when you attempt to stretch tax-deferred retirement accounts, there's always greater risk of not withdrawing the required amount annually and owing a 50% penalty.

3. Funding your retirement. Tax-deferred retirement plan rules were set up to help you fund your retirement. If you plan correctly, you can withdraw income from your plans annually to meet your retirement living expenses. You also can preserve your taxable assets by investing in tax-advantaged funds on the stock side and tax-exempt funds on the fixed-income side, thereby significantly reducing your income taxes owed annually on this portfolio. The alternative minimum tax (AMT) may reduce the tax savings in some situations, so it is important to work with your advisors closely on strategies such as these.

Why use this strategy? Because under the current tax law, retirement account assets inherited by nonspousal heirs do not receive a step-up in basis.

The assets are fully taxable for estate tax purposes, and when received by heirs are also subject to ordinary income tax. By contrast, assets in a taxable account that are inherited by nonspousal heirs do receive a step-up in basis—the cost basis is the fair market value at the time of inheritance.

Hence, it's more advantageous to use your tax-deferred retirement plans to fund your living expenses during retirement, since they currently are subject to double taxation at your death at combined rates as high as 87% (46% estate tax, 35% federal income tax, 6% state income tax), and to manage your taxable account as tax efficiently as possible.

INHERITANCE RULES

When you set up a 401(k) or IRA, a primary beneficiary must be named who will inherit your account and its assets at your death. Most individuals name their spouse, which makes perfect sense since a spouse inherits assets estate-tax-free under the unlimited marital deduction and is likely to need the assets when the first spouse dies.

But designating your spouse may not always be the best choice. In some cases, other heirs may need the assets more than your spouse. Or you may have remarried and may want the assets to pass to your first spouse. Or your spouse may be older or infirm and shouldn't have control of the assets upon your passing. In still other cases, you may want to pass those assets directly to a child or grandchild or a charity rather than your spouse, who stands to inherit other significant assets as well as a sizable life insurance benefit.

When nonspousal heirs are named the primary beneficiaries of your retirement plans, they must follow several inheritance rules under the current tax law—depending on how old you were at death:

- **If you were under age 70½ at death.** Your nonspousal beneficiary has three choices:

  ➤ Withdraw the entire amount no later than December 31 of the fifth anniversary of the year of your death.

  ➤ Or take annual distributions based on his or her fixed life expectancy, allowing for the rest of the account to continue growing tax-deferred. If the beneficiary chooses this option, he or she must take the first distribution by December 31 following the year of your death.

➤ Or take over your life expectancy rate when you died.

• **If you were age 70½ or older at death.** Your nonspousal beneficiary is required to withdraw the same annual amount you withdrew at the time of death.

If a nonspousal beneficiary neglects to choose by the end of the year in which you died to make withdrawals based on his or her own life expectancy rate, he or she is required to take a lump-sum distribution within five years of your death. This is another reason why heirs designated to inherit your retirement plans should be in close contact with your wealth advisor.

INHERITANCE OPPORTUNITIES

Whether you choose at age 59½ to delay making withdrawals from you're your retirement plans or decide instead to live off the income stream, someone still is going to inherit whatever assets remain when you die. There are two tax traps here under the current tax law:

First, if your spouse inherits, there are no estate taxes but when he or she dies, your spouse's estate will probably be larger and more likely to face estate taxes. Second, if nonspousal heirs inherit your retirement plan assets, they will not receive a step-up in basis.

To delay or avoid estate taxes and preserve assets for specific heirs, many affluent individuals designate trusts as beneficiaries or they gift assets. Let's look at some of the most common strategies:

Bypass trust. Also known as a credit shelter trust, a bypass trust is ideal when the size of your estate is significant. Under the current tax law you are allowed to leave an unlimited amount of assets to your spouse, estate-tax-free. But when your surviving spouse dies, only your spouse's estate-tax exclusion will escape estate tax. The amount above that exclusion will face significant estate taxes.

A bypass trust enables each spouse to capture his or her full estate tax exclusion, effectively doubling the exclusion. Under a bypass trust, the surviving spouse controls the distributions of assets in the trust, withdrawing as much or as little as needed during his or her lifetime. When the surviving spouse dies, the trust's assets pass to designated beneficiaries—typically your heirs.

Normally, the bypass trust is set up upon the first spouse's death through his or her will, and the assets remaining in the spouse's retirement plans would pass into the trust. The surviving spouse would then preserve as much of the assets as possible so that upon his or her death, whatever assets remained would pass to the trust's beneficiaries estate tax-free.

If your spouse is not named a beneficiary of the bypass trust, he or she makes mandatory withdrawals each year from the retirement plan assets based on the life expectancy of the trust's oldest beneficiary. If the oldest beneficiary is relatively young, the withdrawals will be lower than if the surviving spouse had withdrawn them, theoretically allowing the retirement plan assets to last longer.

QTIP trust. A qualified terminable interest property trust (QTIP) can be effective when you want both your new spouse and children from a previous marriage to benefit from your retirement plan assets when you die.

Here's how the trust works: Upon death, your retirement plan assets pass into a QTIP trust set up by your will. Your spouse receives income from the trust and withdraws the required minimum distribution each year. When your spouse dies, the assets in the trust pass to the trust's designated heirs— typically your children from an earlier marriage. The assets are counted as part of your spouse's estate.

Without a QTIP trust in place, your current spouse would inherit your retirement-plan assets without owing estate taxes. The problem is he or she would then be free to name beneficiaries—such as a new spouse or his or her children from an earlier marriage. As you can see, without a QTIP trust, children from your first marriage might not receive any of your retirement plan assets.

To sum up, when you die, a QTIP trust will provide your current spouse with income and minimum distributions from your retirement plan assets. Then when your spouse dies, the remaining assets will pass to designated heirs—in many cases children from a first marriage.

Bypass/QTIP. As discussed, the purpose of a bypass trust is to ensure that your estate tax exclusion is preserved when your assets pass to your spouse at death. And a QTIP trust ensures that specific assets pass to designated heirs.

The two trusts often are paired when the value of your estate at death exceeds the exclusion amount sheltered by the bypass trust. Here's how it works: To minimize the estate tax owed, the amount in excess of the exclusion passes into a QTIP trust, which then provides your surviving spouse with income and your heirs with the assets when your surviving spouse dies.

Outright gifts. If you want to divide your IRA assets among several heirs when you die, I recommend setting up separate IRAs for each heir. While you can leave heirs percentages of a single IRA by designating multiple beneficiaries, it's far more efficient to set up separate IRAs and fund them with assets of equal value.

Gifting to charity. Many individuals prefer to leave charities assets when they die rather than gift during their lifetime. If you want to leave assets to philanthropic causes, retirement plan assets are more ideal than taxable assets. Why? When you leave charities cash from a 401(k) or IRA, your estate receives a full charitable deduction, which will eliminate the estate tax on these assets.

Be sure to avoid letting your 401(k) and IRA assets reach your estate before the charitable donation is made. Otherwise, your estate could face income tax on the charitable donation. To avoid this problem, set up two IRAs—one with the charity named as beneficiary and the other with your heirs named as beneficiaries.

SECTION 691(C) DEDUCTION

This deduction is frequently overlooked, and can result in overpaying income taxes. Section 691(c) of the Tax Code was designed to eliminate the unfair double taxation of a retirement plan. Simply put, when estate taxes are paid on retirement plan assets, the IRS does not asses income tax on the full value of the plan—only the difference between the full value and the estate tax paid. This may sound obvious, but you would be surprised how many families miss this deduction and wind up paying millions in unnecessary taxes.

CHECKLIST

1. Inform your wealth advisor of your retirement plan accounts and provide regular updates. This will help your advisor integrate your holdings into your total portfolio, maintain proper asset allocation and rebalancing strategies, and ensure approximate correlation between assets.

2. Know your maximum annual 401(k) and IRA contribution levels and the retirement plan distribution rules.

3. Avoid early withdrawals before age 59½ and don't forget to take minimum annual distributions starting at age 70½. Both mistakes trigger penalties on top of taxes.

4. Know the rules for inheriting retirement plan assets—and which distribution method is ideal for your needs.

5. Use income streams from your 401(k) and IRA accounts to fund your retirement and take steps with your wealth advisor to make your taxable account as tax-efficient as possible.

6. Think twice before delaying withdrawals to stretch an account's tax-deferred status for your children or descendents. Discuss your distribution plans with your wealth advisor and accountant.

7. Consider a bypass and QTIP trusts to preserve IRA assets for designated heirs and to minimize or avoid estate taxes.

8. If you plan to bequest IRA assets to charity and to beneficiaries at death, set up separate IRAs now—one for each philanthropic cause and one for each heir.

5

PROTECTING STOCK OPTIONS AND RESTRICTED STOCK

Ask most senior executives how their companies generate revenue and they will likely tell you which divisions are strongest, why those divisions are producing, and what the company's overall goals are over the coming year.

Ask the same executives about their own stock-option or restricted-stock packages and most will draw a blank. They know they hold stock options or restricted stock. But in almost every case they aren't sure what type of options they hold, how the options or restricted stock will be taxed when sold or when selling makes the most financial sense.

Many of these executives blame the clock, and who can blame them? Senior executives reach lofty levels because they have an amazing ability to focus intensively on near- and short-term business goals, and they devote enormous amounts of time and energy to achieving them. Their longer-term personal issues often take a back seat or are delegated to a spouse, whose knowledge in such matters may be limited. These executives aren't procrastinators or chronic delegators. There are just too many other pressing business matters that absorb most of their time. In many cases they forget to inform their wealth advisors or accountants of their annual option and stock grants—until, that is, after they sell and when it's too late to plan a tax strategy.

Actually, there's another reason why executives let their stock options and restricted stock ride: Studies show most executives view these securities as *free money* and consider them a perk or incentive rather than an integral part of their compensation package. Many of the executives I talk to say they intend to roll up their sleeves and learn the ins and outs of these securities the next time they need to sell them to raise cash. Almost all say they do not factor them into their portfolio allocations or wealth-preservation programs. In other words, they simply hope for the best.

But wishful thinking isn't a financial plan. Stock options not only represent a significant part of your wealth, they also make up a large portion of your annual pay package. If I haven't yet jolted you to action, consider this: A growing number of companies are shifting a larger chunk of executive pay to performance-based equity and away from salary increases. What's more, as corporate boards face increasing pressure from regulatory agencies and shareholders, they are compelling their companies to alter the eligibility, vesting periods and size of incentive packages handed to top executives, making the sell and tax rules more difficult to understand.

In this chapter I will simplify the stock option rules, show how they are taxed, explain incentive stock options, nonqualified stock options and restricted stock, and tell you how to diversify your position.

SIMPLIFYING YOUR STOCK OPTIONS

If you add up the value of your stock options, restricted stock, monthly pay and shares purchased through an employee stock purchase plan, you will quickly see that an enormous part of your wealth and income is riding on one company and that diversification may be needed to reduce your exposure to downside risk.

If you are a senior executive at a major company, the odds are that you hold a significant number of stock options and will probably receive more each year as part of your compensation package. Before we look at the two types of stock options, let's simplify the language a little:

- **A stock option**—gives you the right to buy your company's stock at a specific price within a set period of time.

- **A grant**—is the number of options your company gives you at one time. The *grant price* is how much you will have to pay per share if you choose to buy them.

- **To exercise**—is the action you take to acquire the stock your company gave you the option to buy. When you exercise a stock option, you purchase the stock at the grant price. Once you exercise an option, you take possession of the stock and you can either hold onto it or sell whenever you wish, just as with any security you own.

- **Vesting date**—is a date in the future when you are allowed to exercise the options you have been granted. Most companies set staggered vesting dates for the options they grant. This strategy is used as a carrot to motivate you to improve the company's profitability and stock price over time.

- **Expiration date**—is when the options you were granted are no longer available to you.

I find that most executives immediately understand the meaning of these terms when I use them all in a single sentence: "If your company grants you stock options, you must exercise them between the date they vest and the date they expire."

HOW STOCK OPTIONS ARE TAXED

Now that you understand what stock options are and the terms that are commonly used when referring to them, you should know that there are two different types of stock options:

- **Nonqualified stock options (NQSO)**

- **Incentive stock options (ISO)**

Many large public companies and small closely held ones use NQSOs and ISOs to recruit and retain key employees and to reward them if their hard work improves the company's bottom line and share price over time.

The big difference between the two types of options is how you are taxed when exercising them. Before I explain, you first need to know the meaning of the word *spread*:

- **The spread**—is the difference between your grant price and the market value of the stock when you exercise it. To illustrate, let's say you hold stock options granted at $40 a share. Let's also assume that when you exercise them, the company stock is trading at $50 a share. Hence, the spread is $10 a share.

As I mentioned, NQSOs and ISOs are taxed differently. If you exercise NQSOs, you will owe ordinary income tax on the spread. So, let's say you exercised NQSOs granted to you at $40 a share. And let's say the stock is trading at $50 a share on the date when you exercise them. You will owe income tax on the spread—$10 a share. If you are in the 40% combined federal-state-local tax bracket, you'll fork over $4 a share to Uncle Sam and keep $6.

By contrast, if you exercise ISOs, there is no ordinary income tax owed if you follow the IRS's rules. These rules state that if you do not exercise your ISOs for at least two years after the date they were granted and hold them again for one year and a day after you exercise them, you will owe only long-term capital gains when you sell the shares. Your gain is the difference between the grant price when you exercised the options and the market price when you sold the shares. However, if you exercise or sell before the periods mentioned above, you will be taxed at your much higher ordinary income tax rate.

So, if you were granted ISOs at $40 a share, held them for two years, exercised them, and then held the shares for a year and a day before selling them at, say, $50 a share, you'd only owe capital-gains tax on $10 a share. If you exercised or sold before these IRS time periods, you would owe much more tax on that $10 a share because it is subject to ordinary income tax.

Before you assume that the lower capital gains tax rate on ISOs make them much more favorable than NQSOs, consider this: While the ISOs' spread is not viewed by the IRS as ordinary income, the spread is an adjustment item under the alternative minimum tax (AMT) calculation. That means the ISO spread is counted as a preference item by the IRS for the purpose of calculating your AMT owed.

- **The alternative minimum tax**—The AMT was created in 1969 to ensure that wealthy individuals do not itemize their way out of paying taxes. As I'm sure you know, your CPA always runs your annual income tax numbers using the AMT tables and the ordinary income tax tables. You owe whichever tax is higher—the one using the AMT calculation or the one using the ordinary income tax calculation. Exercising and selling ISOs could cause you to owe the larger AMT.

As you can see, you must know the type of stock options you hold now and will receive, and your accountant and wealth advisor should always be consulted prior to exercising option grants or selling the shares.

You need to know not only what you hold and the best ways to sell, but also you need a plan for funding the exercise of your stock options and a plan for diversifying the proceeds. That's why you must inform your wealth advisor and accountant whenever you're granted stock options or restricted stock and whenever you are planning to sell vested shares.

But before you read another word, I urge you to find out what type of company stock options or registered stock you hold. Then read the sections below that relate to your specific holdings.

INCENTIVE STOCK OPTIONS (ISOs)

Clearly, diversifying a large stock-option position and factoring your option program into your wealth preservation strategy are essential. That means you need a plan in place to carefully time the exercise and sale of your stock options that takes into consideration the rules.

If you hold incentive stock options (ISOs), you face three major IRS restrictions: Your company must require your options to expire 10 years after they are granted to you, you cannot be granted more than $100,000 worth of options that vest in a single year and your options can be transferred at death only to your spouse. To exercise (buy) your ISOs, you have three choices:

1. Pay cash. Here you would simply write a check to your company for an amount equal to the number of vested shares you want to exercise, multiplied times the grant price. So if you want to exercise 1,000 shares and the grant price is $40, you'd write a check for $40,000.

2. Borrow. Here you would take out a loan or borrow on margin the amount needed. To continue our example, you would need to borrow $40,000. Keep in mind that borrowing makes sense only if the cost of the loan or margin is favorable. Your wealth advisor can help you here.

3. Pyramid. With this strategy, you would swap shares of your company's stock that you already own to cover the cost of exercising new options. In our example above, you would need $40,000 to exercise 1,000 options. To pyramid, you would hand over $40,000 worth of company stock you already own to pay for the options you want to exercise. The higher the stock is trading above the options' grant price, the fewer shares you'll need to surrender.

For example, if your company's stock were trading at $60 a share, you would need only about 667 shares to complete the transaction. In effect, you would be trading 667 shares (at $60 a share) for 1,000 shares (at $40 a share). This strategy is particularly beneficial because it's cashless and, in situations like the one illustrated above, you would wind up possessing more shares. The cost basis of your new shares will be the same as the cost basis of the shares you used for the swap.

Pyramiding is ideal when you hold ISOs that are about to expire and want to exercise them, but are short on cash or are reluctant to incur margin debt to raise the cash needed to exercise.

Selling shares after you exercised them requires careful timing. Otherwise you may wind up paying more tax than necessary. You have three choices when considering exercising ISOs:

1. Exercise and hold. In some cases, exercising and not selling shares makes perfect sense, especially in light of the tax rules. Ideally, with ISOs, you want to exercise and hold shares for at least a year and a day before selling. When you hold exercised shares for this duration, your gain upon selling will be taxed at the more favorable long-term capital gains rate rather than your higher ordinary income tax rate.

But this strategy requires cash up front—either out of pocket or a margin loan, or in the form of company stock that can be swapped to exercise the shares. Remember, by exercising you're only purchasing the shares at the grant price. Because in this example you're not raising cash through the immediate sale of the shares, you will need assets to pay for the shares you're exercising and holding.

Exercising and holding exposes you to a major risk: As you hold the exercised shares for a year and a day to qualify for the more favorable capital gains tax, there's always the possibility that the stock's share price will decline and leave you with significantly less value when you sell.

2. Exercise and sell. Most executives exercise ISOs because they need cash for any number of reasons. That means in most cases they will want to sell the shares immediately and use part of the proceeds to cover the cost of exercising the options.

This type of transaction doesn't require cash out of-pocket or a margin loan, and it eliminates the risk that your company's stock price will decline while you hold the shares to qualify for the lower capital gains tax rate. But you will owe income tax due to the immediate sale of the exercised shares, since you did not fulfill the two-year holding period from the grant and the one-year period from the exercise.

3. Give directly to charity. Although ISOs can be transferred only at the death of the employee to a spouse, if the holding period has been met there may be opportunities to gift ISO shares that have been exercised to avoid capital gains tax. In some cases your wealth advisor may decide that holding on to so many exercised ISO shares is not ideal, or that selling them would trigger too much tax. As a result, you may be advised to give the ISO shares to a charity to fund your philanthropic mission. In addition to doing good, you also would avoid the capital gains tax and qualify for tax deductions in the year the gift was made. Be aware, you must be authorized by the company to use ISO shares as charitable gifts.

As for estate planning, many of the restrictions that prohibit executives from transferring ISOs during their lifetime do not exist after death. When an executive dies, all ISOs can be transferred to a spouse, who is free to exercise them immediately without waiting until their original vesting dates. When a surviving spouse dies, inherited ISOs that have not been exercised expire. Hence, you and your wealth advisor should be sure your spouse is completely aware of the various ISO opportunities and risks, as well as the tax consequences of a sale.

Nonqualified Stock Options (NQSOs)

Compared with incentive stock options (ISOs), you have more planning flexibility with the exercise and sale of NQSOs. That's because NQSOs are not subject to the same IRS tax code restrictions. Many of the exercise and sell strategies I mentioned in the section above on ISOs can also be used with NSQOs. But there are big differences:

- **No cap.** NQSOs do not have a $100,000 cap on the value of options that can be granted in a single year.

- **Transferable to heirs at death.** NQSOs are transferable to beneficiaries other than your spouse at death.

- **No expiration limit**. There is no 10-year term limit that your company must impose regarding the expiration of option grants.

- **Tax upon exercise.** When you exercise NQSOs, the spread (the difference between the grant price and market value at the time of exercise) is subject to ordinary income tax.

- **No AMT impact.** When your exercise NQSOs, the spread is not factored into your accountant's calculation to determine if you will owe the alternative minimum tax (AMT).

- **Tax upon sale**. When you sell the shares you exercised, your cost basis for tax purposes is the share price on the date the options were exercised. Let's say you were granted 1,000 shares of company stock at $40 a share and decided to exercise them at $50 a share. You then decide to sell when the share price hits $60. Your cost basis would be $50, and you'd owe long-term capital gains tax on the $10 profit.

Be sure to involve your wealth advisor and accountant when you're granted NQSOs, for tax-planning and wealth-preservation purposes.

RESTRICTED STOCK

In the wake of the accounting scandals of the early 2000s and the corporate governance laws that followed, a growing number of companies are awarding *restricted stock* to senior executives instead of incentive stock options (ISOs) or nonqualified stock options (NQSOs).

Given the range of problems posed by the granting of stock options, more companies are choosing the pay-for-performance attributes of restricted stock. Companies also favor restricted-stock plans because they are easier to manage, they're easier for executives to understand and fewer shares need to be awarded compared with stock options. There are two types of restricted-stock plans:

- **Restricted stock grants**—you receive company stock at the time of the grant and must forfeit unsold shares if you resign from the company or company goals are not met.

- **Restricted stock units (RSUs)**—you receive shares of company stock but can't take possession or sell them until after they vest and other company rules are satisfied. Unvested shares must be forfeited if you resign from the company or if the company's vesting conditions are not met.

How Restricted Stock Is Taxed

When it comes to the taxation of restricted stock, there's good news and bad news. The good news is you're not taxed when awarded restricted stock. The bad news is that when the stock vests, you will owe income tax on the full value of the stock at vesting—even if you don't sell a single share when the shares vest. You'll also owe income tax on all dividends paid in the future after the vesting date.

So, if you were awarded 1,000 shares of restricted stock 10 years ago, when the stock was trading at $40 a share, and the shares vested this year, when the stock was trading at $60 a share, you will owe income tax on the full value of the stock—or $60 a share.

Once restricted shares vest, you can hold or sell them just as with any security. If you hold the shares for a year following the vesting date and then sell, you will owe only the long-term capital gains tax. If you sell before a year elapses, your gain will be taxed at your income tax rate.

While you don't need cash to buy your restricted stock—you own the shares as soon as they vest—you, your wealth advisor and accountant need to do a careful job anticipating and planning for the tax consequences when restricted shares vest, and to decide if you should sell.

Or you can take advantage of Section 83(b). This section of the U.S. Tax Code gives you the choice of paying tax immediately on the restricted stock's value in the year you are awarded the shares rather than waiting until the shares vest, when the stock's market value may be much higher. In any event, sooner or later you are going to have to pay regular income tax on the value of the shares when they vest. The key question is whether you have the money available now to pay the taxes or whether it makes more sense to defer and wait to pay. To qualify for this treatment, you must complete a special form and file it with the IRS within 30 days after the date you were awarded the stock.

The move establishes your cost basis at the date of tax payment and you won't owe tax until you sell shares, regardless of how much your shares grow in value over time. Your tax upon sale will be based on whether you held the stock for a year (capital gains tax) or sold them sooner (ordinary tax rate).

But if the stock price remains flat for years after you pay the tax, you've paid the tax sooner than necessary—in effect giving the IRS an interest-free loan. If the stock price is lower when it vests, you will have paid more tax than necessary. And if you are required to forfeit the stock—because you resign or the company decides to take the stock back—you cannot recover the taxes paid.

Consulting your wealth advisor and accountant is essential when determining whether it's smart to take advantage of Section 83(b), how to cover the tax bill upon vesting and when to sell shares that vest.

DIVERSIFYING YOUR POSITION

As you can see, stock options and restricted stock not only make up a sizable portion of your compensation, they also likely contribute significantly to your net worth. As you now know, you need to inform your wealth advisor and accountant about the type or types of stock options and restricted stock you hold and are awarded. Your wealth advisor and accountant also need to know the vesting schedule of these securities and the company's rules related to vesting, selling and hedging.

But you and your wealth advisor need to discuss another area related to these securities: Whether your stock options and restricted-stock holdings have resulted in too large an investment position in your company. If your position is excessive, you'll need to discuss with your wealth advisor and accountant how to lower your risk exposure and diversify into other assets classes and securities.

You also should discuss how you want these assets to pass to heirs. As I said above, incentive stock options (ISOs) can be bequeathed only to a spouse, while nonqualified stock options (NQSOs) can be bequeathed to whomever you wish. As a result, your spouse and heirs should know what steps are available to them should they inherit your options. Your wealth advisor will need to know who are the beneficiaries of your options, which means your wealth advisor will need to be in touch with your estate attorney as well as your family members.

If you hold NQSOs, it may be advisable to bequeath unexercised options to a trust at the time of death. You'd name an heir the beneficiary of the trust and set up staggered payments over time, leaving the exercise and sale of NQSOs to a financially wise trustee. By doing this, the assets will pass directly to a younger-generation heir rather than to a spouse, and they avoid any estate taxes upon the surviving spouse's death.

The size of your holdings also is an issue. To ease the size of your position, it may be wise to sell options or restricted stock now instead of waiting, and use the assets to fully fund tax-deferred accounts annually and diversify among other asset classes and asset types in accordance with your chosen allocation.

Your position in stock options and registered stock should always be based on your long-term financial goals and the asset allocation model established by your wealth advisor. In all probability, you may need a plan in place that reduces the size of a large position as options and restricted stock vests, and reallocates the proceeds in a diversified portfolio and trusts set up for generational wealth planning.

CHECKLIST

1. Find out what type of options/restricted stock you hold.

2. Get the vesting schedule for your options/restricted stock.

3. Get your company's rules for exercising/selling/transferring.

4. Provide all information to your wealth advisor/accountant.

5. Jointly determine if your option/stock position is too large.

6. Develop a plan to steadily reduce and diversify your stake.

7. Review the tax implications of your exercise/sell strategy.

8. Discuss wealth-preservation strategies with your wealth advisor/estate attorney.

6

CREATING A
BUSINESS-SUCCESSION PLAN

I f you own a closely held business—and about 25 million Americans do—you probably often wonder what will become of your company when you step down or are no longer around to run it. I'll bet each time you start to think about transferring your business to heirs or employees, you start to dwell on the drawbacks and postpone making a decision. Maybe your children aren't quite ready yet to assume control. Or maybe you worry that employees will take the business in the wrong direction, erasing everything you've worked so hard to build up. Or perhaps you don't want to give up control completely, or at all during your lifetime.

But unless you develop a succession plan that preserves your company's value, minimizes taxes owed and protects your family's wealth from economic downturns and even ex-spouses, your business may not survive at all. It's no secret that only a third of family-owned businesses survive from one generation to the next. Without strategic plans in place, your family could face a "shirt sleeves to shirt sleeves" fate—where the person who wore shirt sleeves while building the business from scratch hands it off to family members who cannot run the business or run it down, only to wind up in shirt sleeves themselves.

A smart business succession strategy requires tax planning, insurance policies for emergency funding, and management training for heirs, including steps to be sure children who work for your business have enough time to be emotionally and professional prepared for the responsibility of running the company.

Trust me, a few lines in your last will and testament about who you want to inherit your business is not only insufficient planning, it's dangerous.

In this chapter, I will explain the concepts behind effective business succession planning and help you identify the issues you need to discuss with your wealth advisor:

YOUR FOUR OPTIONS

Business succession planning is ultimately about wealth protection. You need to take steps to ensure that the equity you've built up in your business is not compromised and that your family inherits as much of your company's value as possible, either through a gift or a sale. To reduce this risk to your company's future and your family's wealth, you need to develop plans with your wealth advisor and other professional advisors while you're healthy and active in the business.

In all my years, I've seen many situations where companies wind up sold for a fraction of their value because plans weren't in place to protect families. For example, your $5 million company may grow to be worth $50 million by the time you die. As a result, if you leave the company to heirs in your will, they may actually have to sell off the business just to pay the estate taxes due on your estate. Remember, even if Congress repeals the federal estate tax, many states have an estate tax with rates that are likely to rise to make up the shortfall. I've also seen companies slip into bankruptcy when sold to employees—not for cash but a note for the full purchase price. The employees then lacked the funding necessary to keep the business afloat after your death.

As the owner of a business, you have four basic options when it comes to transferring ownership of your company. The first two choices focus on *when* you want to transfer your business and the second two focus on *to whom:*

- Sell your business during your lifetime.
- Have your estate sell your business when you die.
- Transferring your business to heirs during your lifetime.
- Transfer your business to heirs when your die.

Keeping a business in the family or selling it for top dollar is possible only if you evaluate the strengths and weaknesses of each succession option and identify the most tax-efficient ways to achieve your goals. Once you and your advisors have decided which of these four choices is ideal, the next step is to consider the strategies that will help you achieve your goal while protecting and preserving as much of the business's value as possible.

LOOK HARD AT FAMILY MEMBERS

Whenever you consider transferring a business to family members, openness is critical in the planning stages. You and your wealth advisor will likely need to address a series of issues related to family dynamics, family members' business capabilities, your emotions and the tax impact on you and inheriting family members. Here are the key questions:

- **What are the conflicts?** What are the differences and disagreements that already exist among family members, and what conflicts are likely to emerge once you gift or sell to them? These conflicts may be as simple as a brother and sister having different work styles or two brothers in the company disagreeing on its future direction. Or you may face the more complex issue of a daughter-in-law who works for the business while her husband—your son—does not. How can family differences be patched up in advance through discussions? And how can family members who don't work for the company be compensated if they aren't the direct beneficiaries of the gift or sale?

- **Can heirs handle it?** What are the shortcomings of family members who will take over the business? Are these shortcomings so severe that they would compromise family members' abilities to run the company? Do family members need training or mentoring in areas of deficiency before assuming control?

- **Do they know your intentions?** Have you discussed business succession plans with family members? How actively involved are family members in those plans? Are they comfortable taking control of the business under the framework you have in mind?

- **What are the financial implications?** Have you allotted sufficient time in a business succession plan to take full advantage of trusts? What gift taxes, estate taxes and generation-skipping transfer taxes need to be considered? Do you need to purchase life insurance coverage in case you die and your family needs cash to keep the business afloat while it searches for new leadership or a buyer?

Once you and your wealth advisor review these issues and identify the areas of greatest risk exposure, you need to explore trusts, partnerships and other strategies that can mitigate each one. I have found that the more open you are with your family about your intentions and their wishes, the smoother the process will go and the longer your business and wealth are likely to survive and thrive.

GIFTING YOUR BUSINESS TO HEIRS DURING YOUR LIFETIME

Whenever you plan to gift a business to family members during your lifetime, you need to consider issues related to business succession (the financial issues surrounding the transfer of your company) and management succession (who will assume control and when).

On the financial front, your biggest hurdle when gifting your business to heirs during your lifetime is the gift tax. Under the current unified tax credit, you are allowed to gift only $12,000 annually to each heir or $1 million total during your lifetime without owing the gift tax. The problem with giving a company to heirs is that the value of the business will almost always exceed the annual or lifetime gift-tax level. As a result, you will need to explore ways to gift the business without facing a sizable gift tax.

On the management side, heirs that work for the business will likely need grooming and mentoring. Just because your children seem capable when you head up your company doesn't mean they will fare as well when you're out of the picture. For example, senior managers who seem to get along with your heirs may compete with them for control much more aggressively once you've stepped aside. If family members aren't prepared to lead the company, command employees' respect and hold off executive challenges to their authority, your business will likely suffer.

Business succession plans not only need to be gift-tax efficient but also provide inheriting family members with sufficient time to develop solid business judgment, establish reputations and create a strategic plan for the company's future.

Let's look at trusts and other tax-friendly entities that not only will reduce tax exposure but also give heirs enough exposure to run the company before they actually get their hands on it:

Grantor retained annuity trust (GRAT). This is an irrevocable trust that not only reduces the gift tax you will owe when gifting your business to heirs but also eliminates the estate tax your estate will owe when you die.

Here's how a GRAT works: You transfer your business into a GRAT and in exchange the business funds an annuity that makes annual payments to you over a set time period of your choosing. When the period ends, the trust dissolves and the business passes to the trust's designated beneficiaries—your heirs.

Transferring a business into a GRAT accomplishes three major goals:

- **Gift-tax relief.** Your gift tax is based on the fair market value of the business when you transferred it into the trust—minus the total annuity payments you are expected to receive over the time period you selected. As a result, no matter how much the business appreciates in value over time, you only owe the original gift tax—provided the business remains in the trust and not in heirs' hands.

- **Estate-tax relief.** Since the business is removed from your estate when transferred into the trust, there are no estate taxes owed when you die.

- **Time to train family members.** Since you determine when heirs gain control of the business based on the annuity-payment you've selected, there is plenty of time for heirs to receive all of the training they need and resolve issues related to family dynamics.

That's why when you set up a GRAT, you will want to choose the longest possible annuity period—preferably the length of your life expectancy based on actuarial tables. Here's why: Let's assume you set up a GRAT that has a 10-year annuity term with a 6% annual payment and the applicable federal rate that the IRS uses to assume growth is 5%. Now let's also assume your business at the time of transfer into the GRAT has an appraised valued of $1 million. Over the 10-year annuity period, you will receive $600,000 based on the 6% return. Subtract $600,000 from the value of the business when it was transferred into the GRAT. The residual value of the business in the GRAT for gift-tax purposes will be $463,302 based on the $400,000 remaining after the annuity payout—plus the interest the IRS assumes the assets in the GRAT will earn at 5% over the 10-year annuity period ($63,302).

Now assume that over that 10-year period, the business grows to become worth $10 million. Even though heirs will inherit a business that has increased ten-fold from the day it was transferred into the GRAT, you will owe no further gift tax. What's more, because the business was transferred into the GRAT, it's no longer considered part of your estate, so heirs will inherit that business free and clear of federal and state estate taxes.

Of course, the example above assumes you die in the 10th year of the annuity payment period. But what if you live longer than the term you chose for the trust's annuity? Using our example, when the trust dissolves in the 10th year, your heirs still inherit the business but the original established value of the business—$463,302—returns to your estate. That's why the time period selected for a GRAT is commonly the life expectancy of the business owner.

For example, let's look at Mike, a 62-year-old business owner who set up a GRAT using his life expectancy for the GRAT's term. Let's also assume that the GRAT has a 6% annuity payment and that the applicable federal rate the IRS uses to assume growth is 5%. If Mike's business had an appraised valued of $1 million when he transferred it into the GRAT, Mike will receive a $60,000 payout annually from the GRAT for his lifetime.

Given Mike's life expectancy (determined by his age and IRS mortality tables), the IRS anticipates he will receive a total of $681,330 based on the 6% annuity payments. If we subtract $681,330 from the $1 million appraised value of the business when it was transferred into the trust, Mike will only owe gift tax on $318,670—since that is the amount the IRS assumes will be passing out of the trust at Mike's death to his children, the trust's beneficiaries.

If Mike has not used any of his $1 million lifetime gift tax exclusion, he will not owe any gift tax when the business is transferred to his children but will have to file a gift tax return showing the gift. Now assume that over Mike's life expectancy, the business grows to become worth $10 million. Even though his children will inherit a business that has increased ten-fold from the day it was transferred into the GRAT, Mike will owe no further gift tax.

This is powerful stuff. If the business had been in Mike's estate when he died, Mike's estate would have owed federal and state estate taxes on the fair market value of the business—$10 million. If we assume a 45% estate tax rate at that time (of course, they could be much higher), then Mike would have owed $4.5 million more in estate taxes simply because the business was part of his estate and not in a GRAT.

But by using the GRAT to transfer the business to his children, Mike avoided estate taxes on this asset and saved his children $4.5 million. It is that kind of tax savings that excites me about working with wealthy families, and why wealthy families need to have good wealth management advisors now more than ever. A word of caution: Be sure to have your business carefully appraised before transferring it into a GRAT, so your gift tax discount is accurate for IRS audit purposes. Also, ask your wealth advisor to calculate the optimum annuity payout from a GRAT, and to determine if additional trusts should be set up to receive the business if the GRAT term ends and you don't want heirs to assume control immediately.

In addition, be aware that a GRAT is not an efficient tool if you want grandchildren to inherit your business. That's because the generation-skipping transfer tax (GST) cannot be discounted on assets in a GRAT. If a grandchild is named the GRAT's direct beneficiary, you or your estate will owe the GST on the fully appreciated value of the business at the time it's inherited.

Charitable lead annuity trust (CLAT). This irrevocable trust lets you decide when heirs will inherit your business and minimizes your gift tax owed, erases estate taxes, and makes donations to philanthropic causes of your choosing.

Here's how it works: You set up a CLAT and transfer your business into the trust. The trust then provides one or more charities with an annual annuity payment for a period of time you select in advance. When that period ends the annuity payments stop, the trust is dissolves and the business passes to your heirs free of estate tax.

As with a GRAT, the fair market value of your business is locked in when you transfer it into the CLAT. This means the gift tax owed is based on the value of the business at the time of transfer—minus the total expected annuity payment due to your favorite charities over the chosen time period. No matter how much the business appreciates over time, your gift tax remains the same, based on the original value minus the expected total annuity payments.

If the trust's annuity payment period ends before your death, the value of the business before it was donated to the trust returns to your estate. As for heirs, they gain control of the business when the trust dissolves.

Clearly, getting a comprehensive appraisal of your business before it's transferred into a CLAT is essential. You must be sure that the gift-tax discount you claim is accurate. As for income taxes, you will receive a one-time charitable deduction for the total expected amount that will pass to charity during the period chosen for the annuity. The trust will owe income tax on taxable income after charitable payments are deducted.

In the case of a GRAT or a CLAT, the trustee determines who will run the business. You can serve as trustee, but if you do you must limit your powers in order for the transfer of your business to heirs to qualify for the tax breaks. This requires that steps be taken to ensure that you are not controlling the very asset you donated to the trust. For example, if you want to serve as the CLAT's trustee, you may want to choose a charitable cause in advance for the duration of the trust—or name someone else to select charitable beneficiaries each year.

Ask your wealth advisor about other rules and restrictions that apply in order to qualify for maximum tax-saving benefits.

Family limited partnership (FLP). By transferring your business into an FLP you dramatically reduce your gift tax owed, and there is no estate tax on the business when heirs finally inherit it. The big difference between an FLP and a GRAT or CLAT is that the agreement governing an FLP can be modified. In addition, there are no annuity payments.

Here's an example of how an FLP can work: You can transfer a business into an FLP, and you can retain a 1% *general partner* stake that gives you complete control over the company's management and sale. You then issue the remaining 99% stake as *limited partner* shares, which are held by you and slowly gifted to heirs over time. Limited partners enjoy a percentage of the income generated by the business based on the number of shares held. But they have no say over the company's management or its sale.

When you transfer your business into the FLP, you receive a gift tax discount on the limited partner shares, which typically can run somewhere between 15% and 60% of the value of the business. This discount is subtracted from the appraised value of the business. These shares receive this discount because there is no real market for such securities. Also, you no longer own 100% of the business, and limited partners have limited power to control the company.

When you set up an FLP, you need to establish protocols that ensure you won't run afoul of IRS rules. In recent years, the IRS has targeted FLPs that have claimed excessive gift tax discounts based on inflated values of the donated business. The IRS also has cracked down on FLPs where the person who transferred the business is still determining how much income he or she will receive from the company, or who benefits financially from the business. The IRS has been explicit in how much say you can have over an asset donated to an FLP that receives preferential tax treatment. If the IRS determines that its rules have been violated, the business will be considered part of your estate, and gift and estate taxes will be owed. Two steps to minimize running afoul of IRS rules:

- **Get a comprehensive appraisal.** Having your business appraised by a competent and respected firm that specializes in the valuations of partnerships and business interests is vital. In some cases, you may want two appraisals to ensure verification of the company's value. This will ensure that the gift tax discount you're claiming is legitimate and not inflated.

- **Set clear lines of control.** Accounting books and records should be carefully maintained, and distributions should be in accordance with IRS rules. In addition, regular meetings should be held between all partners, and business assets must be kept separate from the personal assets of the donor. Problems arise if you continue to remove income and make decisions without the consent of all partners.

One of the best ways to ensure that business control issues do not arise with an FLP is to create a trust—such as a GRAT or CLAT—and name an independent trustee. In this scenario, you would transfer your general partnership shares into the trust, and the trustee would decide whether to accumulate income from the business or make distributions to partners. The trustee would also monitor your administration of the FLP.

I worked recently with a husband and wife who wanted to transfer their $10-million pipe manufacturing business to their two sons. The couple was in their early 50s and wanted to remain involved with the business for another 10 years. Both sons worked for the company and wanted assurance from their parents that if they stayed with the business they would one day inherit it.

The parents, however, didn't want to lose control of the business immediately, or pay a substantial gift tax if they gifted the business to their sons. So we set up an FLP that named the parents general partners and established limited partnership shares that did not have voting rights and could not be sold for 25 years without unanimous agreement of all limited and general partners. This move made the limited partnership shares highly unattractive to anyone other than their two sons, since owning those shares did not come with the right to control the business, vote on business matters or sell the business. As a result, the limited shares were illiquid, noncontrollable assets.

The couple's plan was to gift the limited partnership shares to their sons over time. Remember, the FLP owned the company, so the couple was indirectly gifting interest in the business through the limited partnership shares, but the sons couldn't control the company, vote on company business or sell the company.

According to IRS rules, if you receive interest in an asset that you can't control or sell—in this case, the limited partnership shares—the asset is not worth a dollar-for-dollar value, which as you recall was $10 million in this situation. Instead, we were able to value the company at about 30% less, or $7 million. This means the parents would have had to pay a gift tax only on the $7 million discounted value, not the $10 million appraised value.

Now, if the FLP could be extended for another 20 years—meaning the sons wouldn't gain control, vote or sell during that period—the parents would get an even bigger discount for gift tax purposes. So the couple took another step. Instead of gifting the limited partnership shares directly to their sons, they gifted them to a grantor retained annuity trust (GRAT).

This trust was set up to last 20 years and pay 5% a year in the form of an annuity. Now, if the company was worth $7 million when it was transferred into the FLP, and they retained an annuity when the FLP was transferred into the GRAT at 5% for 20 years, the couple will receive 5% of $7 million, or $350,000, a year for 20 years. At the end of 20 years, when the trust dissolved, the limited partnership shares would pass to their sons.

Let's do the math. By setting up and funding only the GRAT, the couple would have received $350,000 a year. But by setting up and donating the business to an FLP, they owe gift tax only on $7 million. By putting the FLP's limited partnership shares in the GRAT, the business is no longer worth $7 million. It's worth $10 million minus $7 million—the value of what they will retain in their annuity ($350,000 x 20 years).

The result is that for tax purposes, the couple's business is now worth $3 million. Under the current gift tax law, the husband is entitled to a $1 million lifetime exemption and the wife is entitled to the same. As a result, only $1 million in gift tax is owed on this large gift. However, planning techniques such as these are complex, and you must work closely with your wealth advisors. You need to determine if it is worth paying the gift tax now to take advantage of the growth that will occur in the business knowing that there will be no estate taxes owed later. A husband and wife still control the future of the business as general partners, and their sons will inherit the business without owing estate tax upon the couple's death.

Because the FLP's limited partnership shares are in the GRAT in the above example, the trust, and not the couple, receives the $350,000 annual annuity payment and the FLP owns the business. As managers of the business, the couple decided that the trust would pay the annual $350,000 to the limited partner, which as you recall is the GRAT. Hence, the $350,000 was returned.

Limited liability company (LLC) is a business entity with limited liability—meaning it protects members' interests against claims by creditors, litigants and former spouses. Like an FLP, an LLC is revocable, meaning that you can change the agreements governing it. Like shareholders in a corporation, members are not personally liable for the activities of the LLC. Like partners in a partnership, the parameters of one's ownership interest are governed by an operating agreement.

An LLC can either be *member-managed*, where each member has equal rights in the management and operation of the LLC, or *manager-managed*, where a manager or managers specified in the LLC agreement are given the right to manage and operate the LLC. In addition, an LLC could have voting and nonvoting membership interests, in which case the LLC is managed by the voting members or a managing member designated by them.

With an FLP or LLC, the donor of the business can retain control over both the management of the underlying assets and distributions to heirs. When you transfer limited partnership interests (FLP) or nonvoting membership interests (LLC), you retain control over the business and reinvest cash flow rather than making distributions to members.

In addition, because there are substantial transfer restrictions on limited partnership interests and nonvoting membership interests, they are nonmarketable and can't be readily converted by the beneficiary into cash.

As in the case of the FLP's limited partnership shares, an LLC's membership interests can be placed in a GRAT, CLAT or other trust for the benefit of heirs, resulting in protection and tax savings.

SELLING YOUR BUSINESS TO HEIRS DURING YOUR LIFETIME

If you want to sell your business to heirs during your lifetime, one way to do so is through a private annuity. A private annuity lets family members purchase your company in installments without a significant capital outlay. The payments for the sale are made to you in the form of an income stream for life.

This strategy is most financially appropriate when there is a great likelihood of early death due to terminal illness and near certainty of a significant estate tax.

A private annuity provides heirs with the means needed to buy your business and eliminates estate taxes, transfers appreciated property to heirs estate-tax-free, and defers your capital gains taxes. With a private annuity, you calculate a fair market valuation of your business and apply the appropriate discounts based on your lack of control and lack of your shares' marketability.

However, if you outlive your life expectancy, you could wind up overpaying for the interest. That's because the IRS uses specific tables that state how much has to be paid to ensure that the sale is not a gift transaction.

Another big danger, of course, is that if heirs fail to make the business a success and the business goes bankrupt, your income stream from the private annuity would dry up.

TRANSFERRING YOUR BUSINESS TO HEIRS AT DEATH

If you want heirs to inherit your business, transfer the business during your lifetime, not at death through your will. There's simply no tax-efficient way to transfer a business through your will. I see many families inherit a business when the owner dies, only to face estate taxes up to 50% of the estate's value. That's because a business is typically held in the form of corporate stock, and if that stock is in the deceased's name, the stock becomes an asset in his or her estate. I've also seen instances where the business owner did not have life insurance to cover the cost of these taxes, and did nothing to discount the value of the business during his or her lifetime. As a result, the family had to sell the business just to meet the tax obligations of the estate.

A better way to pass a business to heirs at death would be to name a charitable lead trust in your will as the beneficiary of your business. The trust would then be structured to pay a charity a steady income stream for a set number of years before the trust dissolves and the business passes to heirs, free of estate taxes. But if you're going to set up such a trust, you're better off doing so during your lifetime so you can prepare heirs for the transition.

SELLING YOUR BUSINESS TO EMPLOYEES DURING YOUR LIFETIME

A business owner typically sells a business to employees when he or she does not have heirs, or heirs cannot, or do not want to manage the business. Selling your business to employees also may make sense when employees are better suited than heirs to run the company.

If you plan to sell your business to employees, the key question is how the employees will pay for it. They either can buy the company using normal operating cash flows, or they can create investment vehicles to build up a capital base that allows them to buy you out.

In a majority of cases, a business is sold to employees on one of two ways:

Employee stock option plan (ESOP). An ESOP allows employees of a closely held business to buy your company's stock by paying cash or having money deducted from their paychecks. Ultimately, your position in the company is bought out, and the business is transferred to employees, who hold majority stock positions.

There are two ways an ESOP can generate the funding needed to issue shares. The ESOP can borrow money from a bank, or your business can make contributions to the ESOP—or a combination of the two. Cash from the loan is then used to buy your shares.

After the ESOP borrows cash to buy the shares, your company makes a tax-deductible contribution to the ESOP to repay the loan. Contributions to the ESOP are tax deductible at the company's marginal rate.

Then the ESOP allocates shares to individual employees' accounts based on compensation or seniority. Employee shares can vest immediately or over a period of time, depending on the ESOP's rules.

However, there are a few drawbacks to an ESOP. First, ESOPs are costly to set up—about $30,000 for the simplest plan. And if new shares are issued, the stock of existing owners will be diluted, an occurrence that must be weighed against the ESOP's tax benefits. Second, when employees resign or retire, the company must buy back employees' shares at their fair market value, which can be expensive.

A company also must be evaluated carefully to determine the price of its shares in the ESOP. I knew a 68-year-old man who owned an advertising agency that he had to sell. He didn't have children to pass the business to, so he sold it outright to two key employees. Unfortunately, the capital gains tax on the sale was substantial, leaving the owner with much less than he had hoped to walk away with from the sale.

Had he set up an ESOP to allow the two key employees to purchase the business from him, he could have taken the proceeds from the buyout of his shares and reinvested the assets in U.S. stocks and bonds; the new shares would have qualified as *replacement securities*. This means that he would have been able to defer his capital gains tax and kept all of the proceeds to invest. By selling his business directly to the two employees, he grossed about $5 million but had to pay about $1 million in taxes. ESOP rules provide business owners with an incentive, when they sell their companies to employees, to take the proceeds and invest them in the private sector. That means the proceeds can't be in invested in municipal bonds, international stocks and any other security outside of the US private sector.

Installment sale. This strategy involves employees purchasing your business through installment payments over a period of time. The big advantage here is that your capital gains tax is due only as payments are made to you—not all at once. The benefit to the buyers is that they do not need to come up with the entire payment at once. In fact, the installment payments can be financed through profitable operations of your business.

SELLING YOUR BUSINESS TO A THIRD PARTY DURING YOUR LIFETIME

In most cases, when you sell your business to individuals who are not your employees, or to another company, you likely will be required to remain involved with the business for a period of time following the sale. Typically, you will receive a percentage of the sale up front, with the remaining portion paid out based on your ability to retain clients and expand the business over a period of years. Buyers of your business will expect you to fulfill this role as a way to ensure continued growth of the business during the transition of ownership, and to hedge against the risk of the business foundering soon after you depart. You also may be required to retain shares of the stock issued as part of the sale for a set period of time.

Be aware, however, that new owners typically change the direction of a business—either by putting their own people in charge, who have a different approach, or by integrating your business into theirs. This could have a negative impact on earnings, leading to losses or collapse. As a result, you need to weigh how payment for your business will be made and the terms of your continued employment at the company. Discuss with your wealth advisor whether cash upfront for your business or partial payment in equity is preferred.

Another way to pass along your business to a third party is through a charitable remainder trust (CRT). This irrevocable trust is ideal when you want to transfer your business in exchange for fixed income for life, receive a sizable tax deduction and fulfill philanthropic goals. Here are two of the most common CRTs and how they are used:

Charitable remainder annuity trust (CRAT). You donate your business to this irrevocable trust. The trustee (which could be you) sells the business to a third party and reinvests the proceeds for greater returns. There is no capital gains tax on the appreciated value of the business at the time of sale. You receive fixed payments from an annuity funded by the sale's proceeds. Whatever assets remain in the trust at the time of your death are passed to one or more charitable organizations named as the trust's beneficiaries.

Charitable remainder unti-trust (CRUT). This trust works similarly to a CRAT, except the assets in the trust—whether that's the business or a portfolio set up with the proceeds from the sale of the business—is revalued annually and the income you receive is variable instead of fixed, based on portfolio's value. This trust is ideal for someone who desires more income as the trust's value increases, can tolerate investment risk to achieve growth and wants to make additional gifts to the trust.

One big drawback of any CRT is that the assets pass to a charity upon death, leaving heirs without inherited wealth from the business. This drawback can be overcome by using life insurance and an irrevocable life insurance trust (ILIT) in combination with the CRT. When you set up the ILIT, you take out an insurance policy that will replace the value of the business gifted to charity. You place the policy in the ILIT, and upon death the charity receives the CRT's assets and heirs receive the insurance policy's death benefit—without estate taxes owed.

But you don't have to put 100% of your business into the CRT. I worked with a family in Hawaii that owned a lucrative clothing business. The owner wanted to sell the business, which was worth more than $20 million. The capital gains tax on the sale would have been steep—about $3 million to $4 million.

I asked the owner of the business if he would consider a charitable remainder trust. He said he didn't want all of the proceeds from the sale to go to charity. So we told him that he could put 25% of his company's closely held stock in a charitable remainder trust (CRT) and keep 75%. The portion that the CRT would sell would not be subject to capital gains tax. The 75% stake that he kept would face capital gains tax when sold, while the assets in the trust would pass to charity when he died. When he funded the CRT with his clothing store stock, he received a charitable income tax deduction for the full 25%—or about $5 million. That reduced his capital gains tax owned on the sale of his 75% stake to less that $1 million.

He never realized that he could put portions of his business in a CRT. With some of the proceeds from the sale, he bought a paid-up insurance policy through a life insurance trust, with a death benefit that would pass to heirs who didn't receive the $5 million that passed to charity.

As you can see, there are many technical rules that will need to be addressed by your wealth advisor.

Selling Your Business to a Third Party at Death

Some business owners want to run and control their companies throughout their lifetimes. They avoid trusts so they are free to draw income depending on their taxes and expenses. In such cases, the owner usually decides that when he or she dies, the family will sell the business to a third party.

But if you plan to sell your business upon death, you need to take steps in advance to ensure that your family receives full value for the company and isn't hamstrung or compromised by unforeseen problems. Here are two strategies to make sure your family is able to sell the business for full value when you die:

Buy-sell agreement. A buy-sell agreement is set up during your lifetime with another individual or company. This third party agrees to buy your business for an agreed upon price when you die or are incapacitated. Such an agreement typically removes the threat of disputes among family members after you die. A buy-sell agreement also establishes the value of your interest upon death for estate tax purposes. There are three types of buy-sell agreements:

- **Cross-purpose agreement**—allows surviving shareholders to purchase your interest upon death or disability at a price set by the agreement. Funding for the purchase comes from the shareholders, not the company.

- **Corporate redemption agreement**—allows the company to buy your interest upon death or disability at a price set by the agreement. The company provides funding for the purchase.

- **Hybrid agreement**—combines both the cross-purpose agreement and corporate redemption agreement. Here, the company or the surviving shareholders have first rights to buy your business interest—depending on how the agreement is written.

Buy-sell agreement with insurance coverage. In my opinion, a buy-sell agreement is virtually worthless unless it is protected by a life insurance policy. Why? If you die, a buy-sell agreement merely states that a third party will buy your stake for a specified amount. But what if your business is facing hard times—or the third party can't come up with the funding to complete the transaction?

A life insurance policy provides a cash stream, giving your family time to sell at the best price possible. The cash might be used to keep the company afloat or hire management to run the company longer until a buyer willing to pay fair market value is found. It is important to have the business comprehensively appraised and to make sure the life insurance policy covers the appraisal value and not just the contract price. If the buy-sell agreement is drafted properly, it will also contain a provision tied to an appraisal value. I have seen some real tragedies when the buy-sell agreement contained a fixed price that was well below the value the IRS determined the business was worth at the time of death. In one case, even though the wife of a deceased business owner received the contract price of $2 million for the business, she owed $6 million in estate taxes. As a result, she had to sell estate assets to pay those taxes because there weren't sufficient assets to fund the buy-sell agreement.

An employee stock option programs (ESOP) and an installment sale could also be set up to allow the company to pass to employees when you die, either through stock or through installment cash purchase.

PROTECTIVE MEASURES

No matter what business succession plan you select, you need to discuss with your wealth advisor appropriate steps to protect your plan against ex-spouses and heirs in need of cash flow. For example, if your business has issued shares to heirs, those shares need to be protected from divorce attorneys seeking assets and from family members who may be inclined to sell.

A defensive move includes a life-insurance-backed buy-sell agreement that removes sell decisions from heirs' hands, plus agreements that state who can own shares, how and when the business will be transferred to heirs and how and when other family members can buy shares back. You also can set up *voting trusts*, which hold shares and assign voting rights and dividend distribution rights to trustees.

CHECKLIST

1. Decide with your wealth advisor whether to transfer your business during your lifetime or at death.

2. When transferring during life, decide whether to gift or sell your business to heirs, employees or a third party.

3. If gifting to heirs during life—evaluate their business skills and impact on family dynamics. Then consider a GRAT, CLAT, FLP or LLC to minimize gift taxes, avoid estate taxes and delay the transfer.

4. If selling to employees during life—consider an ESOP or installment sale.

5. If selling to third party during life—consider a CRT or installment sale.

6. When transferring at death, decide whether to bequest to heirs or sell to employees or a third party.

7. If selling to employees or a third party at death—consider a life-insurance-backed buy-sell agreement.

7

NAMING A
DURABLE POWER OF ATTORNEY

Few things in life happen the way we expect them to. A debilitating health crisis such as a stroke or heart attack can strike at any time. Tragic accidents also occur when least expected. In some cases victims recover fully or partially from life's random blows. In other cases they are unable to function for extensive periods of time before recovering or deteriorating.

While you can't predict such events, you can protect your wealth from this uncertainty by giving one or more persons or institutions the power to make financial decisions on your behalf if you're incapacitated and cannot act for yourself. If someone isn't given durable power of attorney over your financial affairs, your wealth could be tied up in court for years as family members struggle for control and financial institutions refuse to comply with family wishes based on legal grounds.

In this chapter, I will tell you about the different types of durable powers of attorney and strategies to use when selecting your agent.

DURABLE POWERS OF ATTORNEY

Some affluent individuals skip the formality of appointing durable powers of attorney because they fear that giving anyone wide-ranging control over their finances could lead to abuse, which is certainly possible. They also falsely assume their spouse can handle these types of matters if they are incapacitated. But unless you officially grant your spouse durable power of attorney, he or she will be able to perform only a limited number of tasks—such as signing checks and withdrawing cash from joint financial accounts. These tasks will typically be governed by the forms that were signed when the account was created, and not by state law.

Without a durable power of attorney, your spouse would be prohibited from selling jointly owned securities or other property without your signature. Your spouse also could not rename the beneficiary of your life insurance policy or change the beneficiary of your retirement benefits. This is due to the fact that the spouse has no legal authority to act for the incapacitated spouse without being appointed by the court to act as legal guardian. In addition, the judge would have to agree to allow your spouse to be your guardian. There is always the chance that your children or others will contest your spouse serving in this role. Clearly, just a few days delay in appointing a guardian for your property could be costly. Your spouse could be prevented from accessing needed assets to buy an asset, or from taking quick action to sell assets, which could cause big losses or missing out on significant financial opportunities.

As you can see, if you do not provide one or more agents with durable powers of attorney, your wealth will be inaccessible to those who need to make decisions on your behalf and your wealth will be exposed to downside market risk. Clearly, the time to draw up a durable power of attorney and name one or more agents is now, when you're healthy and active.

In this chapter, I will explain the different types of powers of attorney available to you, when to use them, and how to take steps to ensure that your wealth and your wishes are protected.

POWER-OF-ATTORNEY BASICS

All powers of attorney are revocable—meaning you can change agents or void the type of document you hold and replace it with another. There are two general types of powers of attorney:

Ordinary power of attorney lets the person you name conduct your personal, business, legal and tax affairs while you're healthy. Why would you do this? Business or personal trips may cause you to be out of the country or unavailable when critical business documents must be signed or personal financial decisions made. Normally, the powers under this type end if you become incapacitated or die. There are two drawbacks: No enforceable guidelines exist to govern how these powers are used. In addition, a simple power of attorney cannot shield the person you name as your agent from a court challenge.

Durable power of attorney (DPA) lets the person you name conduct business for you when you're healthy or incapacitated. The durable power of attorney terminates when you die. In this category, there are two types of durable power of attorney:

- **A general DPA** gives your agent authority to act in all of your financial affairs—including banking, borrowing, selling property, accessing safe-deposit boxes, paying for support and care of family members, filing tax returns, dealing with property, handling legal claims, hiring financial professionals and making gifts outlined in trusts.

- **A limited DPA** restricts the person's powers to certain specific types of business or is in force only for a set period of time. You also can limit the agent's powers to certain business transactions and prohibit others. This type of DPA might be used if you're away on business and unavailable or incapacitated. Or you may want to use this one when you do not want the agent chosen to make decisions on your behalf while you're healthy. As you can see, the document is flexible and must clearly spell out types of tasks the person may perform and when. You also need to clarify how your incapacity will be determined so that when your agent uses the power of attorney on your behalf, he or she will be able to convince the third party that you are debilitated. Generally, incapacity means you are impaired due to mental or physical illness, mental deficiency, advanced age or other factor that causes him or her not to understand or communicate to make decisions.

MAKING THE RIGHT CHOICES

Many affluent individuals make the mistake of thinking that a power of attorney is a straightforward estate document that's drawn up, signed and stored away. In fact, there are twists that need to be addressed with your wealth advisor and other professional advisors to be sure you've selected the right agent and that he or she has full power to act on your behalf. Let's look at what you need to discuss with your wealth advisor:

Select the right agents. In order for a durable power of attorney to function as designed, the person or people you choose as your agents should be honest, have good judgment and be able to handle your affairs or know where to turn for help. Personally, I recommend selecting people who have a high level of integrity, regardless of how financially astute they are. I have found that if an individual is fundamentally honest, that person is more likely to do what's best for you and your family. And that person can always consult with your wealth advisor and hire all of the accountants and attorneys necessary to provide input on matters involving the affairs of your estate. Make sure this person is familiar with your thoughts and ideas about all of your financial affairs.

Review your state's laws. Before you have a durable power of attorney document drawn up, ask your wealth advisor to confirm who is legally allowed to be named as your agent. Some states allow only a family member to serve in this capacity. In other states, a court-appointed guardian, conservator or committee can overrule your durable power of attorney agent.

Name co-agents. Instead of naming just one agent with durable power of attorney over your affairs, consider naming two agents. Naming co-agents improves the odds that your financial affairs will be conducted as you wish. If you name only person, for example, he or she may decide to underspend on your healthcare during your incapacitation so heirs can inherit as much as possible. Naming a financial institution as a co-trustee will further guarantee that your wishes are executed as stated and minimize the odds of abuse. Frequently, a bank is named as a co-agent.

Name alternate agents. If one of your co-agents quits, dies or becomes disabled, you will need someone else to assume that agent's responsibility. As a result, you will want to name not only primary co-agents but also at least one secondary successor agent in case one of the co-agents declines the task or cannot perform the function. Typically, individuals appoint a spouse first and then an adult child, a brother or a sister. One also could name a close friend or a wealth advisor as a secondary agent.

Pay agents a fee. People work harder and take greater care when they are compensated for their time and effort. In some cases, your agent may need to devote long periods of time to researching how best to manage your affairs when you cannot do so. The task may even involve travel to review and sign documents or consult with your advisors. To compensate your agents fairly, you may want to include a clause in your durable power of attorney authorizing a set daily fee. You can also set up the document so that agents review any bills submitted, which results in a system of checks and balances to reduce the likelihood of overbilling.

Inform your agents. Many people name agents for durable powers of attorney and then keep those people in the dark. The motive for secrecy often is privacy, or a concern that telling them somehow will increase the odds that the powers will be abused. If you do not inform your primary and secondary agents and your become incapacitated, your agents may not be prepared to take appropriate and necessary steps. In addition, they may not know where to find essential documents. If agents must search for key papers, the result is often delay, an inability to execute investments and other financial documents and a risk that your assets will be transferred to their own financial advisors, who may be inferior to your wealth advisor and certainly won't know your complete financial picture. Ideally you, your wealth advisor or estate attorney should provide copies of the document to all agents.

Write up instructions. Once you inform your agents of their chosen status, make sure they know your wishes regarding your finances should you become incapacitated. The best way to handle this is with a letter of instruction updated regularly, since your wishes can change over time. The letter should state what you'd like done and the order of importance should cash be needed or invested assets need to be sold. You also should include all contact information for your wealth advisor and other financial professionals, should they need to be reached.

Check all institutions. Review the rules governing powers of attorney at all of the financial institutions where you do business. You don't want an institution standing in your agent's way over regulations or policies For example, banks, insurance companies and other financial firms may be reluctant to accept the agent you've named in your durable power of attorney. In other cases, they may refuse to acknowledge agents named in documents signed longer than six months ago. If these documents aren't in place at the time of your incapacity, your agent may be unable to act on your accounts. In many cases, financial institutions have their own durable power of attorney forms that must be completed. For example, if you want your durable power of attorney to allow your agent to interact with the Social Security Administration, Internal Revenue Service and other government agencies, you may need to complete the different agencies' durable power of attorney forms.

Without completing such forms, your agent may wind up having to appeal to financial institutions in writing, along with a guarantee to hold the institution harmless for relying on the agent and indemnifying the institution should any legal action result from relying on the agent. Or your agent may have to sue to gain control of your assets on deposit at financial institutions.

Fighting such institutional battles take time and can undermine the very purpose of a durable power of attorney—to put someone in your place as fast as possible to make financial decision on your behalf and on behalf of your family's wealth.

Consider *springing* powers. In many states, there is an alternative to the durable power of attorney. It's called a *springing* power of attorney. This power becomes active only when you're incapacitated. For example, you may not want another person to act on your behalf while you have the physical capability to act on your own. Ask your wealth advisor if your state allows for such a power of attorney to be drafted and whether it's advisable given your situation and needs.

Review current documents. You want to be sure the right agents are named in your current durable power of attorney. The document you signed years ago may be out of date, or may not grant all of the powers you hoped it would to the person acting on your behalf. I suggest you review your durable power of attorney with your wealth advisor annually.

Include provisions for nontaxable gifts. This provision is important because many durable power of attorney forms don't include the right of an agent to make nontaxable gifts. Why is this important? Let's say you were using your annual gift tax exclusion to reduce the size of your estate. And let's say you become incapacitated just as a grandchild entered college. If you were not incapacitated, you could have reduced the size of your estate by paying your grandchild's entire tuition, gift-tax-free, by writing checks directly to the child's university. You also could have gifted $55,000, under the current tax law, to the grandchild's 529 college savings plan for future use. This lump-sum contribution would be counted as a tax-free, five-year gift made all at once.

Unless you include a nontaxable gift clause in your durable power of attorney, your agent may be prohibited from taking advantage of these and other estate-shrinking techniques. Without a durable power of attorney that spells out the appropriate gift powers of your agent(s), your estate might incur higher estate taxes because tax-free gifts could not be made.

Add trust powers. If you've set up revocable trusts that haven't been funded completely, your agent should be given the power to continue transferring your assets into the trust. Your agent also should have the power to continue your gifts to irrevocable trusts, which typically require annual donations.

HEALTHCARE POWERS OF ATTORNEY

Many states recognize what is known as a healthcare power-of-attorney. This document empowers the person or person named attorney-in-fact to make medical decisions on your behalf. Typically, a healthcare power-of-attorney has a broader scope than a living will, which simply expresses your wishes regarding stopping or not beginning medical treatment that delays your death if you have a terminal condition.

What's the difference between a healthcare power-of-attorney and a living will?

- A healthcare power of attorney allows you to name an attorney-in-fact who looks out for your care. A living will does not provide for an agent to be named.

- Your attorney-in-fact can make any and all healthcare decisions that you cannot make on your own. These conditions do not have to be terminal.

- Your attorney-in-fact can authorize doctors to stop water and tube feeding—if that was your wish. A living will does not permit your doctor to stop this type of feeding if the withdrawal of these tubes would be the only cause of your death.

A healthcare power-of-attorney allows for various responses by the attorney-in-fact in the event of the principal's changing medical condition. For example, if you were injured in a car accident and were considered clinically brain dead, your team of doctors could keep you alive for years using a range of machines and medications. However, by giving someone a healthcare power-of-attorney to make medical decisions on your behalf, the attorney-in-fact could authorize the doctors to turn off the machines or not resuscitate you and extend your life—provided your doctors determined that no medical recovery was possible.

Give careful consideration to the person you're considering naming attorney-in-fact. You may decide that more than one person should be named to consult with your treating physician to determine your medical treatment if you are brain dead or incapable of making those decisions for yourself. Not every family member will be capable of acting in this capacity, so you need to consider who will be able to serve in this role. You also need to name contingent attorneys-in-fact if your primary choices are unwilling or unable to serve.

CHECKLIST

1. Decide with your wealth advisor what type of power of attorney best meets your needs.

2. Select primary co-agents and at least one secondary agent.

3. Inform the agents of their roles.

4. Draft a letter of instruction detailing your financial wishes in case of incapacity, as well as a list of your financial advisors.

5. Check the rules of all financial institutions regarding power of attorney. Some require you to fill out special forms.

6. Add trust powers and a nontaxable gifting clause.

7. Provide a clause that allows agents to be paid for their time and effort.

8. Review current documents to be sure they are up to date and reflect your wishes.

9. Provide copies of your durable power of attorney to your agents and other parties that need to know.

8

GIFTING TO CHILDREN
AND DESCENDENTS

Creating wealth takes planning, discipline and determination. Making sure your wealth is preserved and passes to heirs also requires planning, discipline and determination. Otherwise the assets you hoped heirs would inherit will wind up in the government's hands thanks to three taxes—the gift tax, the estate tax and the generation-skipping transfer tax.

What are the most tax-favorable ways to gift to heirs? There are many techniques—some more tax efficient than others. In this chapter, I will address the tax rules that apply to gifts given to different heirs as well as strategies for gifting in the most tax-advantaged way:

THE THREE BIG TAXES

There are three main areas of taxation that you and your wealth advisor and financial professionals need to be aware of:

- **Gift tax.** To prevent you from transferring substantial amounts of wealth to heirs in lower tax brackets, the IRS under the current law allows you to gift no more than $12,000 a year to each heir (up from $11,000 in 2005)—or $1 million total over the course of your lifetime. Assets that exceed the annual or lifetime level face a heavy gift tax.

- **Estate tax.** To prevent you from passing all of your wealth to heirs in lower tax brackets when you die, the IRS taxes your estate under the current tax law if its taxable value in the year of death through 2008 exceeds $2 million ($3.5 million in 2009). While the federal estate tax is phasing out and will be repealed for one year in 2010 or disappear completely before then, it's important to remember that many states impose an estate tax to make up for lost federal revenue, with rates likely to rise as the federal estate tax declines.

- **Generation-skipping transfer tax (GST).** To discourage you from passing wealth to grandchildren and other heirs two generations removed, the IRS imposes through 2008 a hefty generation-skipping transfer tax on the total value that exceeds $2 million ($3.5 million in 2009).

As you can see, your wealth is virtually cornered by the IRS—unless you and your wealth advisor take tax-efficient steps during your lifetime to strategically pass assets to heirs. Strategic gifting not only reduces the size of your estate—and thereby lowers your estate's estate-tax liability at death—but also shrinks the gift tax owed on assets that tend to appreciate over time, such as a business, securities and real estate.

Heirs also need to be prepared for the taxes. Under current tax law, any property gifted to heirs during your lifetime retains your cost basis. So, if an heir sells gifted securities or real estate, for example, the price you paid originally for the asset (minus a calculated percentage of any gift tax you paid, as well as any expenses) is used to determine the capital gains tax owed.

GIFT-TAX RULES

Under current tax law, the amount you are permitted to gift to heirs over the course of your lifetime is $1 million. The tax rate you're charged on the excess declines from 46% in 2006 to 45% in 2007, 2008 and 2009 and 35% in 2010. To keep tabs on your gifts, the IRS compels you to report any gift that exceeds $12,000 annually and pay the gift tax as you go. Here are the IRS rules outlining tax-free gifts made during your lifetime:

Gifting to heirs. You can give gifts outright to children—provided the annual value of your gift does not exceed $12,000 a year. If the value of your gift in a given year goes over this level, you will owe gift tax on the excess on April 15 of the following year.

Under current tax law, you and your spouse can gift $24,000 combined annually to each heir—and to each member of the heir's family. So, for example, each year you and your spouse can gift $24,000 to an adult son, $24,000 to his spouse and $24,000 to each member of their family. That means an heir's family of four could receive up to $96,000 from you and your spouse, gift-tax-free. For IRS accounting purposes, be sure to set up separate accounts to receive each gift or set up one joint account with everyone's name on it.

Some people try to transfer assets above the annual gift tax exclusion by claiming the amount transferred was a loan. But be careful here: Specific IRS rules must be followed whenever a loan is made to heirs. Otherwise, the IRS will view the transferred assets as a gift for gift tax purposes. Consult your wealth advisor and accountant to ensure that gifts to heirs and their families conform to IRS regulations and that loans meet IRS-mandated obligations.

Gifting to a spouse. Thanks to the unlimited marital deduction, you can give your spouse all the assets you wish during your lifetime without owing gift tax. But there is an estate tax catch. While gifting assets to your spouse will not result in a gift tax, after the transfer your spouse's estate will likely be significantly larger than it was before the gift and more likely to qualify for estate taxes when he or she dies. Consult your wealth advisor before transferring assets or property to your spouse to determine the most tax-efficient way to transfer these assets. In some cases, trusts will need to be set up to minimize gift and estate taxes.

Gifting to grandchildren. Under the current tax law, you can gift a total of $2 million to grandchildren over your lifetime (this rises to $3.5 million in 2009) without triggering the generation-skipping transfer tax (GST). Anything above that level would be taxed at a steep rate that drops to 45% in steps through 2009. Consult your wealth advisor for the annual limitations and the GST calculation.

Gifting to minor children. You can gift assets up to $12,000 gift-tax-free to children under the age of 14 using the Uniform Gifts to Minors Act (UGMA).

It allows you to make a gift in the name of an adult who acts as the minor's custodian. The big benefit here is that the unearned income from the gift is taxed at the child's low level. However, if your gift generates unearned income that exceeds IRS levels under current law, the excess will be taxed at your much higher rate. Any unearned income a minor receives above $1,700 will be taxed at the parents' rate. This is a heavy penalty that's designed to discourage parents from shifting assets to their children to avoid income taxes. In addition, all assets must be distributed outright to the minor, usually at age 21.

STRATEGIES FOR GIFTING

It goes without saying that any gift intended for an heir during your lifetime needs to be carefully evaluated with your wealth advisor. Some people think they can avoid the gift tax by adding an heir's name as a joint tenant to an asset or by paying an heir's creditor directly. Both cases qualify for the gift tax if the value of the assets gifted exceeds the IRS' $12,000 annual exclusion.

Some parents gift real estate to their children while they are alive so they can see them enjoy it and so the property is moved out of their taxable estate. But gifting real estate has a number of traps. For one, under current tax law, real estate does not qualify for the step-up in tax basis that it would receive if the property were inherited upon death. For example, if you were to gift undeveloped land to heirs that originally cost you $50,000 15 years ago and is now worth $500,000, your heirs will owe income tax when the land is sold. That tax will be based on the spread between what you paid originally and the fair market value when sold. By contrast, if an heir had received the land as part of a bequest, the cost basis would be stepped up—meaning that the fair market value at the time of inheritance would be the cost basis, allowing the heir to keep significantly more of the gain. In addition, you may owe gift tax on the value of the property.

Despite the limitations on tax-free gifts to heirs, grandchildren and minors, there are ways to maximize gift giving during your lifetime and reduce the size of your estate:

Tuition payments. The IRS allows you to pay the college tuition bills of children or grandchildren without owing the gift tax or generation-skipping transfer tax—provided you write the check directly to the institution. Books, room and board and other related expenses are not included. The gift tax would be owed only when the lifetime level is reached.

Donations to a 529 college-savings plan or other qualified state tuition program are not exempt from the gift tax—although under current tax law you can contribute $60,000 in one year without owing gift tax by having the sum count as a bunched-up, five-year gift to the heir.

Medical expenses. You can reduce the size of your estate without owing the gift tax or generation-skipping transfer tax by paying the medical expenses of an heir directly to the care provider or care facility. Qualifying expenses include diagnosis and treatment, procedures, transportation for care and premiums for healthcare and long-term-care insurance.

Section 2503(c) Minor's Trust. Many wealthy families want to make gifts to their children when their children are young in order to start reducing the size of their estate. But the problem with gifts of $12,000 a year to young children is that they are not capable of managing that amount of money responsibly. You can appoint yourself custodian of the funds you gift to a young child by making the gift subject to the Uniform Transfers to Minors Act. But under the UTMA, the child can access all of the assets when he or she turns 18 (or in some states 21), which may not be ideal.

To keep the money out of a child's hands until he or she is older, you will need to set up a minor's trust. Once the trust is established, you would make gifts to the trust, and the trustee would invest the assets. Trust documents could be set up to distribute assets to the child at age 25, for example, or could make distributions in phases at different ages.

The problem is that the $12,000 annual gift tax exclusion under the current tax law applies only to gifts where the recipient has a *present interest*— meaning the assets can be used immediately and spent however the child wishes, rather than waiting for this privilege sometime in the future. In order to comply with this gifting rule and qualify for the gift tax exclusion, you must give the child the right to access the assets.

One way to comply with this rule so that your gifts qualify for the gift tax exclusion is to set up a Section 2503(c) Minor's Trust. Under current law, this trust allows you to transfer $12,000 a year for future interest to the minor provided certain requirements are met:

- The trustee must be able to use the trust's income only for the minor's benefit and before the minor turns age 21.

- Trust assets must be invested in income-producing assets, such as stocks, bonds and CDs.

- All undistributed assets and income in the trust must be available to the child for withdrawal on his or her 21st birthday for a short period of time—such as 30 days. If the minor chooses not withdraw the assets at age 21, the assets will remain in the trust for the balance of the term you selected when you opened the trust.

- Gifts to the trust are irrevocable.

- If the child dies before age 21, the trust will be included in the child's estate.

Crummey Trust. Another way to allow gifts to a minor to qualify for the gift tax exclusion is to set up a Crummey Trust. The big difference between this trust and a Section 2503(c) Trust is that the Crummey Trust gives your child the right to withdraw the amount of each gift within 30 days after each gift is made instead of just once when the child turns 21 years old.

Since the right to withdraw the assets begins immediately after the gift is made, the gift qualifies for the gift tax exclusion. If the child does not withdraw the gift within the 30-day period, the withdrawal window closes and the assets remain in the trust until the child reaches the distribution age designated by the trust. You can set one distribution age or you can distribute in phases—a part with the child reaches age 25, another part at age 30, at age 35 and so on, for example.

Even if your child decides to withdraw the assets during the 30-day period, he or she can only withdraw the amount of the most recent gift, not the entire trust. If the child decided to do so, you could halt making annual gifts if you wish.

Combining the two. It is common for a Section 2503(c) Minor's Trust and a Crummey Trust to be combined into a hybrid trust—with the Section 2503(c) Minor's Trust in force until age 21 and the Crummey Trust taking over at that point. This hybrid allows annual gifts to the trust to continue to qualify for the gift tax exclusion after the child reaches age 21.

Qualified Personal Residence Trust (QPRT). A QPRT allows you to pass a residence to heirs at a discounted value. Any appreciation on the gift after it's placed in the trust will avoid the gift and estate taxes.

When you transfer a personal residence into this type of irrevocable trust, you retain the right to live there for a set period outlined in the trust. You continue to live there paying the taxes, utilities and all expenses, and only owe gift tax on the home's fair market value when it was placed in the trust. When the trust's term period ends, the residence and all of its appreciated value passes to heirs, free of additional gift tax or estate tax. At that point, you would simply lease the home from your heirs—the residence's new owners.

One downside is that heirs do not receive a step-up in basis. Instead, what you paid for the house plus improvements becomes the cost basis at the time the house is sold by your heirs. Under the current law, the IRS allows you to place up to two residences in a QPRT, which means you may donate a vacation home to the trust. The IRS allows you to rent out a property in the QPRT but requires that you reside in the property for 14 days or for at least 10% of the days it's rented, whichever is greater. The IRS also allows the trust to hold three months' of expenses for mortgage payments and improvements. Cash in excess of these amounts must be distributed only to you.

What if you sell the residence donated to the trust? You are allowed to purchase another property within the trust. But if you do not use the assets from the initial sale to buy a property, one of two events must occur: Either the trust must dissolve, and the assets from the sale must be considered part of your estate, or you must convert the QRPT into a grantor retained annuity trust (GRAT), which pays you an annuity for a set period (usually your life expectancy), after which the residence will pass to heirs estate-tax-free.

Ideally, the property in question should be one that you expect to appreciate significantly in value over time, and one that heirs will want to keep in the family rather than sell. When heirs inherit the property, the value of the gift received will likely be much higher than the property's purchase price. Be sure you consult with your wealth advisor to calculate a QPRT's estate tax savings, as well as the income tax deductions allowed under the current tax law, such as property taxes and mortgage interest payments.

But there are emotional issues to consider with a QPRT. It may be difficult for you to be no longer considered the owner of your home. In addition, while you may want your children to inherit the home, the thought of them circling the property like vultures before you die, or you being forced to beg to stay, may be disconcerting. That's why vacation homes are most often ideal candidates for a QPRT—or any property that is not your primary residence.

Family limited partnership (FLP). When you place an asset such as a business or real estate in an FLP, you pay gift tax only on the property's fair market value at the time of its donation. Then you control the management and sale of the asset, awarding heirs limited partnership shares. The property passes to heirs upon your death and avoids estate taxes. A comprehensive appraisal of the asset before it is donated to the FLP is important. You also need a trustee to determine whether to accumulate income or distribute it to the partners. If the IRS determines that the wrong valuation was made or that you controlled who received payments, the asset may be considered part of your estate for estate tax purposes.

Private annuities. Here, you sell an asset or interest in your family business to an heir or heirs in exchange for private annuity payments for life. There is no gift tax on the transfer of the asset, because it technically was sold in exchange for the annuity payments. Since the asset was removed from your estate and your life annuity terminates at death, there also are no estate taxes on the transferred asset. A private annuity is ideal if you are reluctant to give up all rights to an asset because you are worried you might need it in the future. The private annuity payments replace that need.

Rolling GRAT (grantor remainder annuity trust). When you set up a GRAT, you select a period of time during which you will receive annual annuity payments. An asset such as a business or property that's transferred into the GRAT will fund this annuity. You will owe gift tax only on the fair market value of the asset on the date you transferred it into the GRAT. Since descendents take control of the assets when the GRAT's annuity period ends, the value of the gift in the GRAT is the current market value of the future interests you are gifting to your descendents. So no gift tax will be owed on the appreciation nor will any estate taxes be due.

But a GRAT is beneficial only if you die before the trust's chosen term expires. Otherwise, the appreciated asset returns to your estate and may face estate taxes when you die.

To solve this problem, you can create a series of GRATs—known as *rolling GRATs*. Here, you set up GRATs with two- to five-year annuity periods. Let's say you establish a GRAT with a three-year period and use the first-year annuity payment to fund a second GRAT with another three-year period. Then you'd use annuity payments from the first and second GRATs to fund a third GRAT with yet another three-year period. You would establish as many GRATs as necessary.

The whole point of the rolling-GRAT strategy is to reduce the risk that the appreciated value of the asset at the end of a GRAT's term will decline.

Ask your wealth advisor about the drawbacks to rolling GRATs, which include increased costs to set up and manage, as well as the risk that the IRS Section 7520 annuity rate could be increased or that the tax laws will change, forcing you to invest at less favorable rates when one of your short-term GRATs expires.

Intentionally Defective Grantor Trust (IDGT). This is an alternative gifting strategy to a GRAT and can be used to transfer assets out of your estate that are expected to produce sizable income and appreciate significantly over time. You owe gift tax only on the fair market value of the asset at the time it's donated. The donated asset is also removed from your estate and therefore avoids estate tax when you die.

Normally, whenever you transfer an asset to a grantor trust, the trust's beneficiary—an heir, in most cases—is responsible for paying taxes on the income generated by the donated assets. But if the trust is structured so it's *intentionally defective*, you are responsible for paying the income taxes, not your heir. Why would you want to pay the tax bill? By making income tax payments, you are able to further reduce the size of your estate without owing gift tax.

Ultimately, the asset has been removed from your estate, so it escapes the estate tax. Heirs inherit when you die, but you pay gift tax only on the value of the asset when it was donated to the IDGT. And you are able to reduce your estate further, gift-tax-free, by paying the income tax on the asset in the IDGT.

Life insurance. By setting up an irrevocable life insurance trust and placing a life insurance policy inside the trust, you ensure that if you die prematurely the trust will inherit the assets, not your estate. If heirs are named as beneficiaries of the trust, your spouse can use the trust's assets to care for the beneficiaries. When your spouse dies, the assets that remain pass to your heirs, free of gift and estate taxes, on whatever schedule the trust dictates.

Another way to use life insurance to pass wealth to heirs and avoid gift and estate taxes is by purchasing large-faced life insurance policies and naming heirs as beneficiaries. But taking out a policy with a significant death benefit would require a huge annual premium. To avoid paying such a premium, you could use *premium financing*, which allows you to take out a sizable insurance policy plus a special loan to cover the policy's premium. You're responsible only for interest payments on the loan, which are considerably less than the premium. At your death, your heirs would pay off the loan using the policy's death benefit, which typically grows to be larger than the loan balance due. The benefit here is that you don't have to use cash to pay for the policy, and your heirs won't owe taxes on the inherited death benefit.

But watch out. Payments on a premium-financing loan are tied to interest rates, so there's always the risk that the amount of your loan will climb significantly even if rates rise only incrementally. To mitigate this risk, consider collateral-gap insurance. This type of policy costs about 3% to 5% of the policy's face value and covers the amount that exceeds the rate payment agreed upon originally. Your wealth advisor can offer advice.

As you can see, each trust is ideal for different situations and different goals. Each has its own set of risks. As a result, you need to discuss with your wealth advisor, accountant and estate attorney the approach that makes the best sense for you, and what assets to give, when gifting to heirs during your lifetime.

1. Preserve your wealth by gifting strategically to minimize the gift tax and avoid the estate tax and generation-skipping transfer tax.

2. Reduce the size of your estate by taking advantage of the annual gift tax exclusion, paying college tuition bills and medical bills directly.

3. Consider a Section 2503 Minor's Trust combined with a Crummey Trust when gifting to minor children.

4. Consider a qualified personal residence trust (QPRT) to pass a residence or vacation home to heirs that's likely to appreciate in value over time.

5. Consider a family limited partnership (FLP) or a private annuity to pass appreciating assets to heirs.

6. Consider a rolling granter remainder annuity trust when an asset you're passing to heirs may decline in value over time.

7. Consider an intentionally defective grantor trust to further reduce your estate by making income tax payments on assets donated to the trust.

8. Consider life insurance and an irrevocable life insurance trust to pass wealth to heirs when other assets in your estate pass to charity.

9

GIFTING TO CHARITY DURING YOUR LIFETIME

As a longtime advisor to wealthy families, I have found that there are three big reasons why affluent individuals give so much to charitable causes throughout their lifetimes. The first is a deep-rooted passion for helping and supporting people who are less fortunate than themselves. The second is a heartfelt obligation to give back to their community—whether that means sponsoring a hospital wing, a university chair or simply gifting to the ballet or a museum. The third is a desire to involve heirs in charitable gifting and impart lifelong financial lessons to younger generations. To be sure, there are plenty of other motives for charitable gifting—including not wanting heirs to inherit more than necessary, for fear that wealth will undermine their drive to work and succeed. But for the most part, the three I mentioned are the big ones.

In this chapter, I will review the tax rules governing charitable gifts during your lifetime, explain how trusts and other tax-advantaged gifting strategies can help you achieve philanthropic missions, and how to enlighten family members about the importance of charitable values and managing wealth.

TAX RULES FOR CHARITABLE GIFTING

Before you make any charitable donation, you first need to consider what assets you plan to give, what type of charity will receive your gift and how much control you want over how the gift will be used.

Under the current tax law, you can gift as much as you wish each year to charitable causes. But for tax purposes, the IRS allows you to deduct only a portion of your donation each year based on the type of gift you're making and the type of charity receiving the gift.

In the eyes of the IRS, there are only two types of donations—a cash gift (a check) and a gift of appreciated assets, such as securities (for example, common stock) and real estate. The IRS also divides charities into two types—public and private. Public charities derive their support from the general public through grants provided by individuals, government and private foundations. By contrast private charities, such as private foundations, do not solicit donations from the general public.

How much you are allowed to deduct depends on your gift and the charity:

Giving to public charities....
- **If you gift cash,** your deduction will be limited to 50% of your adjusted gross income.
- **If you gift appreciated assets**, your deduction will be limited to 30% of your adjusted gross income.

Giving to private charities...
- **If you gift cash**, your deduction will be limited to 30% of your adjusted gross income.
- **If you gift appreciated assets,** your deduction will be limited to 20% of your adjusted gross income.

What if you want to donate a sizable gift to a public or private charity but find you cannot deduct the full contribution in a single year because your adjusted gross income is too high? Under the current tax law, when your charitable contribution exceeds the applicable percentage limit for deduction, the excess can be carried forward and deducted over the five years that follow the year in which the gift was made.

But don't assume that cash always makes the best gift. Sometimes gifting appreciated assets makes more financial sense. When you give cash, you receive a higher tax deduction but you miss a tremendous opportunity to remove assets from your portfolio that will likely grow considerably in value over time.

Why is removing an appreciated asset beneficial? If you were to hold on to an appreciated asset that grows significantly in value and then you were to sell it later in life, you would likely owe a significant capital gains tax. But by gifting the appreciated asset to charity instead, you will receive a tax deduction and avoid capital gains tax on that future sale. And you'll remove an asset from your estate that will balloon over time and could result in a significant estate tax upon death. When you gift an appreciated asset, the charity can sell it to raise cash without owing capital gains tax.

After gifting the appreciated asset, you could take the cash you had intended to give and invest it in a diversified portfolio of investments. Going forward, you could continue gifting appreciated assets annually to charities over time, thereby using charitable gifting as a way to diversify your portfolio—and take additional tax deductions.

Besides selecting the best gifting strategy for your tax needs, you and your wealth advisor should take steps to be sure the charities you want to receive your gifts are in sound financial shape and that the assets you donate will be properly used. I've known many people who gifted assets to a charity only to find out later that it was poorly managed or that the donated assets weren't being used effectively or for the intended cause.

Your wealth advisor also should review the charity's past financial statements and future projects, which could expose potential cash-flow problems. This may be an issue of particular importance if the charity is dependent on project funding, which could compromise the charity's ability to invest sufficiently in its infrastructure.

CHARITABLE GIFTING STRATEGIES

Gifting sizable amounts to charity during your lifetime allows you to support philanthropic causes, receive emotional satisfaction, reap tax savings and accomplish estate planning. But providing charities with gifts directly—through cash donations or appreciated assets—does virtually nothing to influence the values of your children and descendents.

If you want your children and descendents to play a role in selecting charities and directing how donated assets will be used, you will need to set up a private family foundation, donor advised fund or charitable trust, depending on your goals and needs. Your wealth advisor and other financial professionals can help you determine which charitable giving entity is right for you and your family.

Private family foundations. A private family foundation is structured like an independent corporation or trust. The foundation's purpose is to hold donated assets and make annual gifts to charitable causes based on the mutual decisions of the foundation's trustees.

Family members typically are named trustees of the foundation, but outside advisors such as an attorney also can be appointed. Most foundations pay trustees a salary for helping to manage operations—which can range from drafting a mission statement and hiring investment advisors and other professionals to assisting in key operational tasks. Recent IRS scrutiny of private family foundations reinforces the requirement that boards meet strict standards to qualify for tax breaks, including holding regular meetings and keeping careful minutes and accounting records.

The big benefit of a family foundation is its flexibility in setting a philanthropic mission and the ability to change that mission at any time. Also, the foundation and its trustees have complete control of how assets will be used. Many family foundations are structured as a trust to ensure that the board will stick to the wealth creator's original mission or at least consider that mission, but problems can still arise. Over time, tensions among family members can arise over how and when to donate the foundation's assets. That's why it's important that your family's shared charitable values be identified early on and a plan be put in place that establishes the criteria for gifting and a protocol for reaching family consensus.

Two big drawbacks of a private family foundation are that they are expensive to set up—legal fees can run $30,000 or more—and they are time consuming for trustees to manage. In addition, tax deduction limits are lower for a private family foundation than for a similar public supporting organization, and the required annual distribution is much lower, minimizing how much can be gifted each year. However, the IRS provides a tax break to family foundations that include nonfamily members on their boards.

One reason private family foundations are so popular among superaffluent families is that they allow contributions to remain intact and do not require families to immediately identify recipient charities. For example, if you have a substantial concentrated position in your family's company stock, you could donate a block of that stock to your private family foundation and receive a deduction in the year the shares were donated to the foundation. Going forward, you, your spouse and children can determine annual charitable causes and make gifts. This strategy could continue during your lifetime and during the lifetimes of your children and descendents in perpetuity, depending on how well the assets are managed by your wealth advisor.

Two points to keep in mind if you are making annual contributions: First, a foundation must donate at least 5% of its total assets to a designated charity. Second, children can be paid a salary or a fee for the responsibilities they are assuming in selecting charitable causes.

Donor advised fund (DAF). The DAF has become an easier and less expensive alternative to the private family foundation. A DAF not only assumes responsibility for the compliance requirements, staffing needs and costs, but also provides a larger tax deduction than private foundations under the current tax law. Generally, there are three ways to set up a DAF:

- Your wealth advisor can establish a DAF for you with a financial institution serving as the DAF's financial arm.

- Your wealth advisor can establish a DAF with a community foundation that invests exclusively in local charities.

- You and your family can set up a fund directly with one of the more than 600 community foundations in the U.S.

Here's how a DAF works: You make irrevocable contributions to the DAF, and you and your family decide which charitable groups will receive annual donations. Back-office tasks such as paperwork, legal issues, accounting and due diligence are handled for a fee by the financial institution or community foundation that established the DAF. You can even set up a DAF that has your or your family's name on it—such as The John Smith Donor Advised Fund.

Under the current tax law, the IRS views a DAF as a public charity, so limitations on deductibility of contributions are less strict than with a private family foundation. If you donate cash to a DAF, you are able to deduct up to 50% of your adjusted gross income (as opposed to 30% with a private foundation). If you donate appreciated assets, you can deduct up to 30% of your adjusted gross income (as opposed to 20% with a private foundation). DAF's are so attractive in this regard that some private family foundations set up DAFs to donate part or all of their assets just to take advantage of a DAF's more generous tax provisions and reduced administrative and legal expenses.

Another big difference between a DAF and a private family foundation is that a DAF is not required to pay salaries to trustees who are children and descendents. And a DAF does not have the expense of paying an attorney's fee to set up a private family foundation. As a result, a DAF is often an ideal choice for charitable assets that are too small to bother with the cost of drafting and maintaining a private family foundation.

A DAF also may be ideal when you want to donate a valuable collection to charity but still retain control over how the proceeds will be gifted. For example, let's say you own a fine art collection. You could set up a DAF in your name with your favorite charity. Then you would donate your art collection to the charity, which in turn would sell or auction off the collection with the prior understanding that the proceeds would go into your DAF. Then you and your heirs would recommend how the DAF's assets would be invested and how the proceeds would be gifted each year. The charity would charge a relatively small administrative fee. Had you sold the art collection yourself, you would have owed capital gains taxes. Had you given the entire gift directly to the charity without setting up a DAF, you would have received a deduction—but you and your family would have lost control of how the gift or proceeds are used.

The only downside to the DAF strategy I cited is that your tax deduction will be based on the appraised value of your collection when donated to the charity—not the market price your collection receives at auction, which might be significantly higher.

Another benefit of a DAF is that your family is able to control which charities will receive annual donations over time. For example, let's say the charity you selected for DAF donations originally was founded to support a specific cause but that over time the cause changed dramatically—so much so that the cause is no longer one your family wants to support.

If you had originally donated a large lump sum to the charity you no longer would have control over the money.

Here's another example: Let's say you make a lump-sum gift to a university. Now fast-forward 30 years, and let's assume your grandchild or great-grandchild is applying for admission at that university. The university may not remember your lump-sum gift made 30 years earlier. By contrast, the university may be more willing to show favor to your applying family member if donations had been made annually over the 30-year period through a DAF and your family still had the ability to end the annual donation.

Charitable remainder trust (CRT). When you transfer stock, real estate, a business or any appreciated asset into a CRT, income from the asset is paid to you and any other designated income beneficiary for life. You also receive a charitable income tax deduction at the time of the transfer, based on the calculation the IRS uses to determine the residual value of the assets left in the trust at the end of the trust term. The charity named as the trust's beneficiary has what is known as the *remainder interest* in the assets in the trust and does not receive full control of the donated assets until the death of the trust's last designated income beneficiary.

There are two types of CRTs—a charitable remainder annuity trust (CRAT) and a charitable remainder unitrust (CRUT). In the case of a CRAT, the assets you transfer into the trust are used to fund fixed annual annuity payments from the trust to you and any other designated income beneficiaries. A CRUT functions the same way but instead of a fixed annuity, the assets transferred into the trust are used to fund a variable annuity. This means annual payments to you and designated income beneficiaries will vary depending on the annuity's annual performance.

For example, Mike, age 64, puts $2 million of highly appreciated, non-income-producing stock in a CRAT. The CRAT can sell the stock, avoid capital gains tax and invest 100% of the assets in income-producing assets. If the CRAT were created to pay out a 6% fixed annuity to Mike for his lifetime, he would receive $120,000 a year. Based on current life expectancy tables and applicable federal interest rates used by the IRS, Mike will receive a charitable income tax deduction of $775,832 because that is what is calculated to be the residual value of the trust.

If you transfer cash into a CRT, you will face the cash limitation deductions based on the type of charity expected to receive the asset. If that charity is a public charity, you will receive your 50% deduction limitation. If the charity is a private charity—such as a private foundation—you will be limited to the 30% charitable deduction. Given that most people fund a CRT with appreciated assets rather than cash, such donations face the more restrictive 30% limit for public charities or 20% for private charities.

How can your children and descendents help make charitable decisions about assets in a CRT? When you set up the CRT, name a donor advised fund (DAF) or a charitable trust as the remainder beneficiary rather than a designated charity. When you die, assets will pass to the DAF or trust, and your family will have influence over charitable distributions on an ongoing basis.

CRTs also are frequently combined with life insurance policies to provide heirs with the value of the asset donated to the trust. Typically, you would use the CRT's annual annuity payments to purchase a life insurance policy for the value of the asset you donated to the trust. If that life insurance policy were set up in an irrevocable life insurance trust for the benefit of a child or descendent, the policy's death benefit would pass free of gift or estate taxes. So when you die, your charity of choice receives full control of the asset you donated to the CRT while your heirs receive the death benefit from the life insurance policy as the life insurance trust dictates.

Charitable family limited partnerships (CFLP). A CFLP is ideal for assets that are likely to appreciate over time. In exchange for donating assets to a CFLP, you receive the general partnership shares (the management shares), giving you 100% control over how the partnership is run, how it invests the donated assets and how it distributes the partnership funds to the holders of the limited partnership shares. You also have the power to gift limited partnership shares on whatever schedule you wish.

A portion of the limited partnership shares can be given to children and descendents, while another portion is given to one or more charitable causes. As a result, you're able to claim a charitable income tax deduction for the fair market value of the shares donated to charity. Then the CFLP can sell the assets and reinvest the proceeds. Eventually, the CFLP will be dissolved, and the charity will receive its share of the assets.

How does a CFLP differ from a CRT? A CRT provides a guaranteed stream of income to you while you're alive and then passes the trust assets to the charity when you die. The CFLP's income stream comes from distributions from the partnership, rather than through a trust, and payments are at the discretion of the general partner. Also, a CFLP allows you to transfer assets such as closely held stock of a family business or real estate, which aren't appropriate for a CRT. In addition, a CFLP allows for a more aggressive asset reinvestment strategy. But the biggest difference is that a CFLP lets you make distributions to a charity whenever you wish, rather than waiting until the CRT's annuity period ends.

Pooled income fund (PIF). A PIF typically is set up and managed by a charitable cause for the purpose of receiving donated assets. When you donate marketable securities to a charity's PIF, those assets are usually sold by the charity and the proceeds are pooled with other donors' contributions and invested.

You receive your share of income from the PIF's invested assets—or you can name someone else to receive the income. You receive a charitable deduction for a portion of your gift, and you will owe income tax on the PIF payments you receive. When you die, the charity that operates the PIF takes ownership of your share of the assets. Unlike a CRT, which requires your selected trustee to handle all recordkeeping and administrative tasks, a PIF assumes all of these responsibilities.

If you donate assets to a PIF operated by a noncharitable entity—such as a hospital or museum—that entity can give you the option to name a donor advised fund or a charitable trust, or even a charity, to receive the remaining assets at death. This move would keep the donated assets intact and allow your family to have a say in how the assets are distributed.

Charitable gift annuity (CGA). Like charitable remainder trusts (CRT), CGAs allow you to shift appreciated assets out of your estate during your lifetime and receive a charitable deduction for part of the assets' value. You or a beneficiary receives fixed annuity payments for life or a predetermined time period. Upon the death of the last surviving beneficiary, the assets in the CGA will pass to the charity, which uses them to support the gifting program you designated when the CGA was established.

Like pooled income funds, charitable gift annuities are cost-efficient from the donor's standpoint since they don't require an attorney's participation, they don't require annual reevaluation from a certified public accountant and they don't require an annual tax report.

Charitable lead trusts (CLT). A CLT works in reverse of a CRT. When you donate an asset to a CLT, your designated charity receives annual payments funded by the donated asset for a set period of time—usually your life expectancy. Upon your death, the trust ends and the residual assets are paid out to the trust beneficiaries, who can be family members such as children and grandchildren.

As with CRTs, there are two types of CLTs: A charitable lead annuity trust (CLAT) and a charitable lead unitrust (CLUT). A CLAT pays the designated charity fixed annuity payments during your lifetime. A charitable lead unitrust (CLUT) pays the charity variable payments based on the performance of the annuity during your lifetime. Children and descendents receive the donated assets free of additional gift tax or estate tax at your death—even though the assets may have appreciated significantly in value over the life of the trust.

Most people who use a CLT fund it with assets that they expect to appreciate over time, and who currently do not need income. They are more interested in making a charitable gift, avoiding transfer taxes on the assets used to fund the CLT and receiving an income tax deduction for the charitable gift.

For example, let's say Ellen, age 69, funds a CLAT with $3 million of stock in her family's business. She names her church, the American Cancer Society and a local community foundation as the three charities to receive income from the CLT. The CLT is set up so that there is a 3% annuity payout to the charities during Ellen's lifetime. At her death, the stock will be transferred to her family members.

She chose to fund the trust with stock from her family's business because she anticipated the stock would grow significantly in value during the remainder of her lifetime. Funding the CLAT with the stock also allows her to avoid gift tax and estate tax on that growth.

Based on IRS calculations and an anticipated growth rate of just 10% each year, the CLAT offers many benefits: The charities will split $90,000 a year in money paid out from the CLAT until Ellen's death. In the year of the transfer, Ellen will receive an $848,079 charitable deduction from income tax because that is what the IRS determines, based on their calculations and current applicable federal interest rates, will be the total amount of money paid out to the charities during Ellen's lifetime.

Let's assume that at the time of Ellen's death, there is about $2.2 million left in the trust. Her estate will owe estate tax on the gift transferred to family members. Why bother setting up a CLAT if Ellen's estate will have to pay this tax? Look at the estate tax savings if Ellen is correct and the business grows during her lifetime. At a 10% growth rate, the actual residual value of the trust assets at Ellen's death will be about $11.5 million. Using the CLAT, Ellen was able to pass on an additional $9.5 million in assets to her family members free of transfer taxation and to receive a large charitable deduction when she set up and funded the CLAT. If we assume the estate tax rate at Ellen's death was as low as 40%, she still would avoid $3.8 million in taxes just by using a CLAT.

HOLDING FAMILY MEETINGS

If you gift to charity during your lifetime, chances are you are doing so to involve children and descendents in your charitable mission. But setting up private family foundations, donor advised funds or charitable trusts, and involving your children and descendents, requires careful planning. Family dynamics between you and your heirs may be more volatile than you realize.

I have seen families where children who work in the family business resent those who don't. I have seen families where members want as much distance from the wealth creator as possible—either because the busy wealth creator never made enough time for them or because of resentment or a desire for independence on the part of the children. I have even seen families where children without professional advisory assistance assert themselves out of spite or because they lack financial knowledge.

I can tell you from experience that nothing squanders a fortune faster than family feuds. Allowing such poisonous dynamics to linger is bad for family unity and for the family's long-term wealth preservation. The lack of a family mission or shared values eventually causes family members to drift further apart and become disinterested in wealth creation and preservation. Fighting becomes sport—a regular activity. The extent to which your family is involved in charitable causes can only strengthen generational bonds, nurture financial and decision-making skills and reinforce the importance of community and self-sacrifice.

If you fear that heirs lack the ability to make informed decisions about charitable contributions or the management of trusts, ask your wealth advisor for help. A growing number of wealth advisors now organize family summits to open lines of communication between members and to discuss issues related to efforts to fund charitable causes.

At these summits, wealth advisors with the assistance of psychologists help families communicate, establish patterns of mutual respect, resolve lingering conflicts, develop mission statements and develop procedures for the discussion of financial and charitable issues. These gatherings often take place during or at the end of family reunions and generally are divided into two parts:

- Discussion of the family's financial issues and charitable mission.
- Teaching of financial skills to help family members manage charitable assets.

In many cases the first order of business when families come together is to draw up a mission statement, which identifies each family member's personal vision as well as the family's collective charitable goals. Once the mission statement is drawn up and adopted by the family as a whole, the next step typically is a communications workshop that helps family members choose their words and tone carefully, so each member is more receptive and respectful of each other.

The business and educational portions of family meetings are designed to prepare heirs for the management of charitable trusts and the preservation of family wealth. For example, each family member's financial knowledge might be assessed and then improved through seminars and exercises. Next, family members of the same generation might get together to review issues that relate to them. Then, the entire family may meet to review issues in their mission statement. And finally, the family meets to cover issues related to the family's charitable causes or the family's foundation or donor advised fund.

At larger family meetings, *officers* may be elected, including a president, secretary, treasurer and technology officer, who ensures that all maters covered are posted on the family's Web site and that regular updates are e-mailed to all members There may even be private coaching for family members who aren't familiar with finance or claim to have no interest. I have even been asked to attend these meetings and teach family members about wealth planning, so that all family members have some basic knowledge from which to draw from.

Annual meetings empower all family members to spend time together with the expressed purpose of working together to fulfill charitable missions and preserve wealth for future generations.

CHECKLIST

1. Make a list of the charities you want to support and discuss them with your wealth advisor and other financial professionals.

2. Ask your wealth advisor to review and evaluate the charities' missions, managers and financial standing.

3. Estimate the size of your charitable gifts based on your feelings, generosity and estate planning needs.

4. Ask your wealth advisor and accountant to help identify assets that are most ideal for charitable gifting.

5. Ask your accountant to calculate the size of your tax deduction.

6. Decide whether you want to gift directly to the charity or through a family foundation, donor advised fund, charitable trust or other method.

7. Consider including family members in all discussions and decisions related to charitable gifting and management of donated assets.

8. Hold annual family meetings to discuss your charitable mission and enhance the financial skills and harmony of family members.

10

TITLING ASSETS PROPERLY AND TAX-EFFICIENTLY

The wealthier you are, the more assets you are likely to own and the greater the risk that some or all of them are improperly titled based on the wishes outlined in your estate plan or wealth management plan. How you hold title to your assets during your lifetime will determine how those assets are distributed at your death.

Every asset of value (including stocks, bonds, real estate, cars, boats, planes and financial assets) requires a title—a legal document that establishes ownership and, by extension, into whose hands the asset will pass at your death.

But titling assets appropriately for tax planning and inheritance purposes can be tricky. Each title has a different set of inheritance rules, and titling errors can cause property to pass into the wrong hands and wealth to be lost to taxes unnecessarily. For example, an improperly titled residence could wind up passing to one child when your intention was for all of your children to share the asset equally. Or a vacation home may pass directly to a surviving spouse rather than to children from your first marriage.

In this chapter, I will explain the different types of titles, the inheritance rules for each and the trust strategies that can protect your estate from paying excessive estate taxes. By understanding the basics, you will be better able to make sure that your wealth advisor and other financial professionals won't overlook important titling issues.

WHY TITLES MATTER

I meet affluent married couples all the time who have many of their assets titled as *joint tenants with right of survivorship*. Under this form of titling, when one spouse dies the other inherits that spouse's share of the assets tax-free under the *unlimited marital transfer*. This may seem smart at first, since there is no transfer or death tax owed on the death of the first spouse. However, when the surviving spouse dies, the estate may owe a substantial estate tax—leaving children and descendents with a smaller inheritance.

I also meet married couples who have invested a great deal of time and money setting up complex estate and trust plans to minimize estate tax exposure but then neglect to retitle their assets after their estate plans are finalized. For example, a couple may have set up a testamentary trust in their estate plans to be funded with a valuable piece of real estate upon the death of the husband or wife. But unless that real estate was properly retitled, it would not be able to fund the trust.

When I remind couples that assets titled as *joint tenant with right of survivorship* pass to the surviving spouse at death and cannot pass into the testamentary trusts they have paid their legal advisors to create as part of their wealth-management plans, these couples suddenly become motivated to complete retitling plans recommended by their estate planning attorney.

Before you consider or implement a titling strategy for any asset you own with your spouse, you need to consult your wealth advisor, accountant and estate attorney. Typically, there are four basic questions that need to be answered:

1. Will your estate owe estate taxes?

2. Who do you want to inherit your assets?

3. What trusts can be set up to minimize estate taxes owed and pass specific assets to heirs or charities?

4. How must assets be retitled to accomplish your goals?

A COMMON TITLING MISTAKE

Unless your assets' titles are coordinated with your will and testamentary trusts, your wealth management plans are likely working at cross-purposes.

For example, let's say you are married with four children and that at the time of death your estate is worth $4 million. But because many of your largest assets are titled *joint tenancy with right of survivorship*, these assets will pass directly to your surviving spouse when you die—regardless of what your will states. This means that none of these assets will pass according to wishes outlined in your will. At the moment of your death, the law considers the asset immediately transferred to your spouse solely because of the way it was titled.

Based on the way the assets were titled in our example, no estate taxes will be owed when you die under the unlimited marital deduction but your spouse will be worth $4 million plus the value of your spouse's own estate. By not retitling assets, you have missed out on leaving assets to you children or other family members when you die and lost the opportunity to take advantage of the estate tax exclusion, which is $2 million in 2006 and set to rise in 2009 to $3.5 million.

Now let's say your spouse dies a year after you and leaves an estate worth $5 million. Under the current exemption, $2 million of your spouse's assets will escape estate tax. But if your spouse left nothing to charity and did not remarry, up to the $3 million remaining may be taxed (46% is the top estate tax rate in 2006 and 45% in 2007, 2008 and 2009. The result could be a stiff estate tax of about $1.4 million. If your state has an estate tax, it could it could be even higher.

It's tragic, but such events happen all the time.

RULES FOR TITLING ASSETS

I have found that when it comes to wealth management plans and estate plans, many married couples act based on their understanding of past actions—meaning that if they set up trusts in their wills, they will assume that specific property will pass into those trusts upon the death of the first spouse. But the surviving spouse often is shocked to learn that the assets cannot pass into the trusts because the assets were never retitled.

This is precisely why wealth management plans and asset titles should be reviewed annually with your wealth advisors and estate attorney. Tax laws and tax rates change. Or your family may have changed. Or you may want assets to pass to different heirs. Or your net worth may have soared and you may need to take additional measures to protect and preserve your wealth. Generally, all of your property is titled in one of the following ways:

Sole ownership. When you are the sole owner of an asset, you can sell or gift the asset during your lifetime without the written permission of others, or you can distribute the asset after you die through your will.

Joint tenancy with rights of survivorship (JTWROS). This title is one of the most common forms of ownership in America today, particularly between married couples. The title lets you own an asset jointly with one or more people. When you die, your share passes directly to the asset's surviving owner(s) regardless of what your will states.

A common mistake many couples make is thinking that an asset held as JTWROS will allow their ownership share to avoid estate taxes. It will not. This is true only when the joint tenant is your spouse. Otherwise, the value of your share in property held as JTWROS is included in your estate at your death and may be subject to gift, estate and generation-skipping transfer taxes. (Exceptions to the gift tax rule include securities, bank accounts and savings bonds.)

Another mistake many people make is adding a child's name to an asset held as JTWROS. I see this most commonly when a when an older person has added a child's name to an investment account so the child can help manage the assets in the account. What the parents either forget or failed to realize was that the child named as a joint tenant will inherit all of the assets in the account when the parent dies—regardless of whether the will states that all the children should inherit the account's assets equally.

For example, let's say your investment account holds $1 million in stocks and bonds, and your will says that when you die the account is to be left to your two sons and a daughter equally. This would not be possible if one son held title to the account with you as JTWROS, since your son will own 100% of the account when you die.

Imagine the anger this will create among the other siblings. Your son could not just give the other siblings $333,000 each because he would be making a taxable gift, meaning your son would be required to use some of his $1 million lifetime gift tax exemption. This mess is all the result of improperly titled assets.

An asset held as JTWROS avoids probate at death, which saves estate expenses and avoids inheritance delays. But the title is less efficient when there are more than two owners of an asset. In such cases, no individual will have sole ownership or control of the asset or how it will be managed. For another, a creditor of a co-owner can seek to possess the entire asset, regardless of the other co-owners' stakes. For example, if a child named as a joint tenant of an asset with two other owners injures someone with a car, the injured party's attorney could seek to claim 100% of the asset as part of damages.

Many couples also assume incorrectly that if an asset is held as JTWROS, they don't need a trust for the asset because it will pass directly to the surviving spouse upon the death of the first spouse. But a JTWROS simply controls who must inherit an asset upon death; it cannot prevent a surviving spouse from leaving the inherited asset to a new spouse rather than to an intended heir, or from selling the asset

For example, if you divorce your spouse, remarry and then die, your new spouse may want the inherited asset to pass to children from a first marriage rather than your children from your first marriage.

Tenants in common. Assets titled *tenants in common* are owned jointly by two or more people. If you are one of these owners, you can sell or gift your share to anyone you wish during your lifetime without the permission of the other owners. When you die, your share of the asset passes to the beneficiaries named in your will—not the asset's other owners. The beneficiary can be an individual or a trust.

The important concept to remember here is that unlike JTWROS, your will determines who inherits your share of the asset.

By naming children in your will to inherit your assets held as *tenant in common*, they will receive only your share of the asset, not the shares held by your spouse or other owners of the asset. Or a testamentary trust can be named to inherit the asset, ensuring that the asset ultimately passes to beneficiaries.

Titling an asset *tenants in common* is especially beneficial when more than two people own an asset such as a vacation home that's used at different times of the year. Since each of the four tenants in our earlier example would own 25% of the asset, if one tenant dies, that person's 25% share would pass to the beneficiaries named in that tenant's will, not to the co-tenants. The other three would continue to own shares and use the home, but they'd be sharing with a new tenant.

Tenancy by the entirety. This type of ownership is similar to JTWROS but it is between spouses. When spouses own an asset jointly under this title, neither spouse can sell or transfer the asset without the other's approval. When one spouse dies, the surviving spouse automatically receives sole ownership. The difference between this title and JTWROS is that one spouse cannot legally undermine the other's right unless both agree to sever ownership.

Community property. Prior to this point, we have talked about property ownership that dates back to *common law*—the laws we inherited from the English system that the colonists brought with them when they founded our country. Community property is a concept that emerged later and was not widely adopted throughout the country. This form of property ownership exists only in a handful of states—Arizona, California, Idaho, Louisiana, Nevada, New Mexico, Texas, Washington and Wisconsin—and affects married couples.

The rules of community property state that:

- Assets you acquired before marriage belong to you alone even after marriage.

- Assets accumulated while married are considered community property—which means you and your spouse own equal shares in the property.

- Gifts given specifically to you or an inheritance you receive after marriage are owned separately by you.

Generally, all property and income acquired during the marriage is owned in equal shares by each spouse. Exceptions to this include property acquired before marriage and gifts or an inheritance received by an individual spouse. All property acquired during marriage is presumptively common. If property owned before the marriage is sold at a profit, the profit is separate (in most states) provided it is kept separate from the community property.

However, the income derived from property (such as rents and dividends) is considered community assets. If separate property commingles or is combined with community property, it becomes community property if it is difficult to determine which is which. This is why I always tell people in community property states that if they think they may face the unfortunate situation of a divorce, they should keep separate property separate and never commingle it. Keeping property separate requires careful bookkeeping, but the effort will be worthwhile if there is ever a divorce.

Contract property. Although *contract property* is not technically recognized as a legal title, there are certain assets that are subject to contractual distribution at death. For example, qualified retirement plans that designate a beneficiary, IRAs with a designated beneficiary, life insurance policies with a designated beneficiary, and any account that is registered as *payable on death* (POD) or *transferable on death* (TOD) are considered to be forms of contract property. When the owner dies, these assets pass automatically to the designated payee or designated beneficiary and are not bound by provisions in a will—unless the designated beneficiary of the contract property is the estate of the decedent, which is often not advisable for tax reasons.

TITLING AND DURABLE POWER OF ATTORNEY

How your assets are titled will determine who can make important decisions about your assets on your behalf, if you are unable to do so because you are traveling or because you are mentally incapacitated. That is why I advise people to have a durable power of attorney (DPA) that allows your agent named in the DPA to act for you if you cannot act for yourself. If you know you are going to be traveling on an extended trip, a limited power of attorney can give your agent limited rights to do specific duties for you, such as sign real estate documents for a closing on a specific piece of property.

But your agent's role will depend on how assets are titled:

- Property you own solely or jointly as *tenants in common* or *contract property* can be managed by the agent of your durable power of attorney.

- Property you own as *joint tenancy with rights of survivorship, tenancy by the entirety* and *community property* can be managed only by the asset's joint tenant—usually your spouse or a trustee—and not by the agent of your durable power of attorney.

If you are worried about how assets would be managed should you become incapacitated, you can set up a revocable living trust and transfer in the assets, which will then be managed by the trustee.

TITLING ASSETS FOR TRANSFER AT DEATH

When you die, your assets pass to inheriting parties based on how your assets were titled. Generally, assets are distributed one of four different ways at death:

1. Probate. Assets that qualify for the probate process must be court supervised and court approved before being distributed. There are three types of assets that pass through probate—solely owned assets, assets held as *tenants in common*, and any *contract property* or trust assets payable to the decedent's estate. In these cases, your will dictates the distribution of assets. If a will does not exist, state laws of intestacy govern distribution.

2. Direct transfer. When you have an asset held in *joint tenancy*, your share automatically passes to your surviving joint tenant, who in most cases is your spouse. Such assets include property held as *joint tenancy with right of survivorship (JTWROS)* and *tenant by the entirety*.

3. Contract beneficiaries. Certain contract assets such as retirement accounts, life insurance policies and annuities pass directly to parties you've named in the contract as designated beneficiaries, regardless of what your will may instruct.

4. Trust beneficiaries. Assets in a revocable *living trust* bypass the probate process and pass directly to designated beneficiaries at death. You set up this type of trust during your lifetime, and you can act as your own trustee if you want to retain management and control of the trust's assets. You also can name a trustee or co-trustee to manage the assets if you become incapacitated.

A living trust is commonly used as a substitute for a will, since the trust provides for the distribution of trust assets upon death. Assets are distributed directly to the trust's designated beneficiaries, and there is no court supervision or probate process. As a result, the passing of assets through a trust generally is faster than through a will.

A living trust is ideal when you want assets to pass to specific heirs without facing legal challenges during your lifetime or having the trust's contents become public record after you die. While assets transferred into a living trust are included in your estate and subject to estate taxes, you can minimize taxes owed by naming a spouse as beneficiary to qualify for the unlimited marital deduction—or by preserving the uniform tax credit when assets pass to a nonspousal heir.

TAX IMPLICATIONS OF TITLES

It is important to remember that no matter how assets are titled—either as *tenants in common* or JTWROS—they will be included in your gross taxable estate at death, which means estate taxes may be owed.

For this reason, many affluent families have their attorneys draft wills that establish testamentary trusts at death to receive property and minimize estate taxes owed.

But many people aren't aware that assets titled JTWROS cannot pass into trusts established by your will. Why? By law, those assets pass directly to the joint tenant and not through your will. Only solely owned assets or those titled *tenants in common* pass through your will and, in accordance with your will, into the testamentary trust.

Assets considered *contract property* such as retirement plan assets also do not pass through your will. At death, they pass directly to your designated beneficiary. Consult your wealth advisor and other financial professionals to determine whether naming a trust as the primary beneficiary of contract property makes sense for your estate plans.

TITLE REMINDERS AND RISKS

All of the strategies I've outlined will be meaningless if your assets are titled incorrectly. Remember, assets titled as *joint tenants with rights of survivorship* (JTWROS) cannot pass into a trust established by your will at death. They will pass instead directly to the asset's co-owner, usually your spouse. Contract property passes directly to your primary beneficiary. Only solely owned property and assets titled *tenants in common* can pass into trusts set up by your will.

If your will already establishes trusts at death to receive assets, you must retitle the assets that you want to fund those trusts.

One way to ensure that you retitle assets destined for these trusts is to have your wealth advisor work with you and your attorney to create a list of assets and their appropriate titles. Then he or she can call or e-mail you monthly to verify that you've retitled the assets appropriately and that copies of the new titles are sent to his or her office as well as the office of your estate attorney and accountant.

Going forward, you and your wealth advisors should examine how your assets are titled, which assets may need to be retitled and whether the trusts set up by you will are sufficient to accomplish your estate plans and wealth preservation goals.

You also should discuss the risks of changing titles. For example, your share of assets held as *tenants in common* can be attached to litigation launched by third parties such as creditors, ex-spouses and litigators. Such a move is much more difficult when assets are held as JTWROS because the litigant would have to wait until you gained complete control of the asset, which could be far off in the future.

Here are key questions to ask when meeting with your wealth advisor and planning professionals on this issue:

- What's the most tax-efficient way for each of my assets to pass at death?

- What are the risks associated with holding assets as *tenants in common*?

- Should trusts be named the primary beneficiary of retirement plans and other contract property to accomplish estate planning goals?

- Does my will need to be amended so new trusts are established?

- Which assets need to be retitled so they conform to my updated estate plans?

CHECKLIST

1. Provide your net worth to your estate attorney and review your current estate plans.

2. If there are no changes to your estate plans, review the ownership titles of assets to be sure they conform to your plans.

3. If your estate plans must be updated to reflect changes in net worth, newly acquired assets, estate tax implications and inheritance goals, consider setting up trusts to protect your estate from excessive estate taxes.

4. Verify that jointly held assets are titled correctly to comply with your new estate plans and testamentary trusts.

5. Make a checklist of assets that need to be retitled and ask your wealth advisor to remind you on a monthly basis until the changes are completed.

6. Review the primary beneficiaries of your retirement accounts.

7. Provide your wealth advisor and other financial professionals with copies of all updated asset titles and beneficiary forms.

11

NAMING THE EXECUTOR UNDER YOUR WILL

Even if you follow all of the advice I have outlined so far in this book, your efforts to expand and protect your wealth may be wasted if you name the wrong person as the executor of your estate. An executor is responsible for managing your estate at death as well as ensuring that assets are distributed as stated in your will and in accordance with the law.

Sounds simple enough, but trust me, there's a hornet's nest of emotional and legal issues that typically emerge following an affluent individual's death. These issues not only can create friction where none existed in the past, but they also can tie up bequeathed assets in court for years. In some cases, such delays can be financially devastating to the individuals or charities you wanted to inherit them. In other situations, extended delays can harm the value of invested assets that are untouchable as competing heirs and beneficiaries work out their differences.

Given my experience with many affluent families over the years, I am convinced that most individuals, given a chance, would replace their executor if they knew what transpired after their death. There are many reasons for executor problems after death: The executor originally named may have been the ideal person for the job when the will was drafted years earlier but now may be completely inappropriate for a range of reasons, including age, infirmity, conflicts of interest or distance from the assets in the estate. Or the original executor may have been informed of the task at the time of appointment but years later forgot about the role and no longer wants the responsibility. And then there are the many disputes that break out over how the person named executor handles the estate—issues that could have been anticipated but were ignored because the deceased party was focused on other matters when alive.

Selecting the right executor—or co-executors if you choose to have more than one—and reconsidering the individuals or corporate entities already named are very significant decisions for you and your family that can have major ramifications on your distribution plans at your death. You must work closely with your wealth advisor and other financial professionals to consider who to name an executor, and successor and contingent executors.

In this chapter I will explain the general tasks an executor must perform, who is ideal to serve in this role, what you can do to ensure that all is handled properly and what duties the executor must handle and how soon after death.

Role of the Executor

Generally, an executor must perform a series of broad tasks related to probate—the legal process that occurs after death to ensure that individually owned property and assets held as *tenants in common* pass appropriately to heirs and entities named in a will. These after-death tasks by an executor include:

- Locating the will and notifying beneficiaries.
- Filing the will with the appropriate courts.
- Appearing in court proceedings and signing any legal documents.
- Creating a list of assets and their values.
- Paying debts, expenses and taxes.
- If necessary, canceling utilities, services and credit cards, and closing accounts.
- Notifying Social Security, Veterans Administration, insurers and any other concerns to initiate benefit payments.

- Hiring and managing professionals, such as an accountant.

- Filing and paying taxes, including estate taxes.

- Getting appraisals for assets such as real estate, collections and artwork.

- Providing for dependents until the will is settled.

- Managing assets that remain after debts, expenses and taxes are paid.

- Distributing assets as dictated by the will after debts, expenses and taxes are paid.

- Keeping family members informed as the estate is settled.

SELECTING AN EXECUTOR

As you can see, the choice of an executor for your estate must be made with care. The individual or institution you select can make a big difference between assets passing smoothly and families remaining on good terms—and assets being held up by litigation and a lifetime of family bickering. Let's look at the benefits and drawbacks of appointing family members and institutions:

Appointing family members. Choosing an executor obviously is a highly personal matter. That's why most people select a close family member—usually a spouse or adult child. But choosing one person has risks. The person may lack experience or the time to perform the administrative tasks. Or the person could become incapacitated or die, creating animosity among family members. Or the person may lack objectivity, which is crucial to the task of an executor.

That's why many people name two family members as co-executors. This way, one family member can ensure that the other performs the task properly—and if one decides to drop out, the other can complete the administrative tasks.

What if there's only one person who's appropriate? You may want to consider naming a family member and financial professional as co-executors. Many affluent individuals I have worked with follow this approach because of the complexity of their estates. The benefit of naming a family member and a financial professional allows the family to be involved in the process but ensures that the family member has expert and knowledgeable support. In addition, an experienced financial professional is likely to advise on the most effective way to communicate with all family members. This is important. When an executor fails to communicate to all family members where inheritances stand, family members often assume they are being personally slighted or that financial trouble is brewing. Charges of impropriety and extended delays typically follow.

If you select a family member or two members, they should be in harmony with your wishes and have a high level of integrity and common sense. Someone with integrity is less likely to steal assets from your estate to pay off personal debts, gratify spending desires or settle grudges. This type of illegal activity is more common than most people think. A person with integrity and common sense can always hire advisors to help make key decisions—such as how to invest assets—even if that person is not financially astute.

The person you choose also should be relatively objective when it comes to family dynamics. Many families have factions that harbor grudges against other factions or resent specific family members. You don't want to choose someone who may want to financially punish a family member who divorced, for example, or hasn't communicated with family members as often as the executor may have wished. The person you choose should be diplomatic and willing to treat all family factions fairly while executing the wishes outlined in the deceased person's will. When an executor appears to favor one faction over another or fails to communicate with all factions, aggrieved parties quickly turn to litigation, and the wishes in your will may be ignored or delayed as these issues are ironed out in court.

Other factors to consider when choosing an executor or co-executors include the person's health and commitment. If your choice becomes ill or infirm, your estate may not be able to transfer assets to heirs until the courts choose a new executor. How much time an individual can devote to the many administrative executor duties needs to be a consideration, not only when you name this person but also over the years when you review your estate plans.

Appointing an institutional fiduciary. To ensure objectivity in the event of divorce or remarriage, some people name business partners, or institutional fiduciaries to avoid the highly charged problems that can occur when members of different families square off over inheritances. The reason for such an appointment isn't necessarily to protect against financial impropriety, as it is to establish a detached, neutral party. In many situations, just the appearance that a family member serving as an executor isn't adhering to the decedent's wishes in a timely fashion can result in litigation, which only slows the passing of assets and interferes with the decedent's wishes.

But institutional fiduciaries come with risks. Not all institutional trustees have been adequately trained or have kept up with their training or the tax laws, which are complex and ever changing. As a result, it is wise for you or your wealth advisor and other planning professionals, such as your attorney, to carefully evaluate an institution before naming it to serve as executor of your estate. Generally, an institutional executor should be granted the power to write checks from your estate to cover its professional obligations. An institutional executor also should be financially strong and able to restore funds to the estate if a mistake is made or there's negligence on the part of the officer handling the estate. You don't want an institutional executor that's in poor financial shape and won't make restitution if it files for bankruptcy. Although institutions charge executor fees, these fees are normally competitive with other similarly sized institutions and are usually based on the size of the estate. The fee schedules are easily obtained from an institution, but I would not base my decision to hire the institution as executor solely on one's fees but on the services provided and the institution's financial standing.

Narrowing Your Selection

Deciding whether to name family members, a financial professional, an institution or a combination takes careful consideration. You can always change your executor at any time with your estate attorney, and many people change executors several times over the course of a lifetime as their families and wealth evolve. Here are factors that may help you narrow your choices:

Consider your DPA agents. Many people choose the same family members serving as agents of their durable power of attorney to be executors of their estate. This often makes perfect sense, since both tasks are administrative and require the same level of integrity, objectivity and adherence to your wishes outlined in your estate plans.

Name contingent or successor executors. As discussed, to ensure that your estate is executed swiftly and in accordance with your will, it's a good idea to name two people as co-executors. But you also should name three or four successor executors who will assume the role of executor if one of your co-executors becomes unwilling or unable to continue to perform the task. These are also sometimes known as contingent executors. Think of successor executors as players sitting on a bench ready to go in for a player pulled out of the game.

Inform executors of their role. The person or persons you name as executor should want to serve in this capacity. This is very important. If the person declines to perform this role at death, a successor executor will be called upon to serve. The successor executor who steps into this role may not be ideal at the time of your death or may cause a range of problems already discussed.

The people you plan to name as executor or successor executor should be informed of your decision prior to the will being signed, and of their role and responsibilities, and they should have an opportunity to discuss the position with you and to accept or decline. Keeping your estate's executors in the dark because you don't want them to feel imposed upon or aware of your personal affairs only increases the risk of trouble. Instead, they are more likely to perform well if they have at least one talk with you about why you are naming them, where important documents are located and how you want your affairs handled. Even better would be a series of talks about your estate and your assets and how things should be done.

Inform executors of your paperwork's location. All individuals named as executors and successor executors need to know where your estate documents are located in the event of your sudden death. In many cases, you only may need to provide them with the name of your estate attorney. Or you may want to provide them with a copy of your estate plans. These documents include your will, your living will, durable power of attorney, healthcare proxy, trust documents and copies of vital papers such as deeds and insurance policy contracts. If you have safe-deposit boxes, tell your executors about them and where to find the keys.

Inform the executor of your wealth advisor. Be sure the person or entity you've named as executor knows about your relationship with your wealth advisor and other financial professionals. Executors who are unaware that such relationships exist will likely transfer the financial affairs of your estate to their own professional advisors. These advisors may not be aware of your estate's complete picture, or may not be as sophisticated or strategic as your wealth advisors and financial professionals. You may even want your will to include specific language directing that your wealth advisor be retained by your estate or trust after you die.

Write a letter of instruction. Even if you have named the best possible executors and successor executors, they may not be fully aware of your wishes on a range of issues not covered by your will. A letter of instruction simply outlines who is to be notified in case of your death, where key documents are located, a list of your key financial advisers and their contact information, and your personal preferences regarding funeral and burial arrangements. This letter also can include your wishes for you children's care, schooling, healthcare needs, gift-giving plans and any other information. You also may want to express your wishes regarding handling of assets and other things in easy-to-understand terms. While such a letter has no legal standing, I have found that the more heirs understand about your wishes, the more likely they are to respect them and execute them without fuss or delay.

For example, if your letter of instruction does not explain why you are leaving one child a particular asset or why you want your child to continue attending a particular school, family battles may break out among members who believe they are best interpreting your will and doing what you would have wanted. A letter of instruction erases doubt and makes crystal clear what you wish.

An Executor's Tasks

No matter how well organized your estate plans are and how smart and informed your executors are, I have found that when someone dies, panic and sorrow set in and executors tend to forget or delay what they're supposed to do. In many cases, the delay is due to being unaware of what must be done. Here's a list of tasks an executor needs to complete in the weeks and months following a death:

In the first week...

- Request multiple copies of the death certificate.
- Locate documents related to assets, debts, taxes owed, financial matters and estate plans.

- Contact the deceased's attorney, or hire one, to handle estate matters.
- Contact the deceased's wealth advisor for a list of other professionals.
- Contact the deceased's wealth advisor, accountant, life insurance broker and any investment brokers for copies of documents.
- Open safe-deposit boxes and review contents with help of surviving spouse or attorney.
- Evaluate how much annual income the surviving spouse will receive from current and inherited assets.
- Prepare a budget of monthly expenses for the surviving spouse.
- Review all insurance policies.
- Encourage the surviving spouse to update estate documents.
- Change vehicle registrations to the new owner's name.
- Help the surviving spouse file for Social Security, death benefits, survivor's benefits and Veteran's Administration benefits.

In the first month...

- Complete probate filing requirements after consulting the attorney.
- Apply for a federal tax ID number for the estate.
- Recover the decedent's mail if there is no surviving spouse.
- Review and pay decedent's bills if there is no surviving spouse, after consulting the attorney.
- See if any life insurance was provided through credit cards.
- Change the name on credit cards, and cancel cards held solely in the deceased's name.
- Contact health insurance providers to change the name on policies and continue coverage for the surviving spouse.

In the first nine months...

- Hire an appraiser to evaluate all property. Provide the accountant with a copy of the signed appraisal for future tax needs, such as the sale of a property.

- Estimate all taxes owed and file returns when due—usually nine months after death.

- Consult the attorney about how to distribute inheritance assets.

CHECKLIST

1. When choosing your executors, consider parties who have a high level of integrity and common sense.

2. Review the parties serving as agents of your durable power of attorney. They may be ideal as executors.

3. Name two executors, to divide the tasks and provide checks and balances.

4. Name successor executors who will serve if one of your executors cannot.

5. Write a letter of instruction clearly outlining your wishes. Include a list of your financial professionals and their contact information. Be sure the letter is accessible to your executor.

6. Consider an institution as co-executor if you have divorced or remarried, to ensure objectivity.

7. Review your executor and successor executors annually and make changes if executors have moved away, are in poor health or are no longer suitable for the position.

—————12—————

DISTRIBUTING WEALTH TO BENEFICIARIES AT DEATH

In the preceding chapters, I have covered three broad categories of wealth management—creating and growing wealth, protecting and preserving wealth, and planning the distribution of your wealth during your lifetime in the most tax-efficient way possible.

Now I want to tell you about a fourth component—planning the distribution of wealth remaining in your estate at the time of death. Just to be clear, this area of wealth management is not an either-or proposition to be weighed against the distribution of wealth during your lifetime. You don't decide to do one or the other. Both are essential for wealth preservation. For example, you may choose to distribute some of your assets during your lifetime to children, descendents and charities out of the goodness of your heart or to reduce the size of your estate, or both. But other assets—such as your IRA, homes and other securities and property—are likely to be held throughout your lifetime, winding up in your estate at the time of death.

Unless you take steps during your lifetime to ensure that remaining assets pass to your family as tax-efficiently as possible and that controls are in place so your beneficiaries use the assets as you intended, the wealth your family inherits could be eroded unnecessarily by taxes and uncontrolled spending whims.

You also will need plans in place if you want some or all of the assets remaining in your estate to be used for special health care needs of an ill or physically challenged spouse or child. Or you may need controls in place to ensure your beneficiaries receive their inheritance at different points in their lives rather than all at once, preventing them from spending it all at once when they are young.

Many people arrange for distributions to be made to young beneficiaries at various stages in life—such as one-third at 25 years old, one-third at 35 years old and one-third at 45 years old. Other people set conditions for family members to continue receiving distributions, such as continued employment, drug or alcohol-free living or greater awareness of money management issues. Or you may want to control how the assets will be invested after you die. As you can see, creating plans for the distribution of assets remaining in your estate at the time of death will preserve and protect family wealth.

In this chapter, I will show you how assets in an estate pass to beneficiaries under a will or trust at death, the estate or transfer taxes these assets may face when you die, and the planning strategies that minimize taxes and allow you to control and extend inherited assets after death.

How Assets Pass at Death

Before we explore the most tax-efficient ways to pass assets remaining in your estate to other parties—and how to control how assets are paid out to those who inherit them—let's look at the different ways assets pass when you die. As you will see, much depends on how your assets are held at the time of death:

Titled assets. Titled assets left in your estate at death are owned either solely by you or jointly with one or more parties. They pass one of two ways:

- Property owned solely or jointly as a *tenant in common* or as community property pass based on the instructions in your will.

- Property owned as *joint tenants with rights of survivorship* and *tenancy by the entirety* will pass directly to the property's joint tenant—regardless of what your will instructs.

Contract property. This type of property includes qualified retirement plans such as 401(k)s, individual retirement accounts (IRAs), life insurance proceeds and annuities that have survivorship rights for another party. Contract property will transfer at death to the parties you've named as beneficiaries—regardless of what your will says.

Assets in a revocable living trust. This is a trust you set up during your lifetime. You can name yourself or another person as trustee. Assets that you use to fund the trust can continue to be controlled by you, and you can dissolve the trust anytime you wish during your lifetime. When you die, depending on how the trust was drawn up, the property remaining in the trust can either pass outright to designated beneficiaries or can remain in trust for the benefit of your spouse and descendants. The main drawback of any revocable trust, of course, is that the assets in the trust at death will be considered part of your estate for tax purposes, even though the assets will not be included in your estate for purposes of probate.

A revocable living trust is set up for three purposes:

1. To enable assets to avoid probate, which can save legal and court expenses.

2. To keep the terms of inherited assets private. When you die, the terms of your will and the assets that pass through your estate are all in the public record because the will must be probated. By contrast, a revocable living trust does not go through probate, so nothing in the trust is of public record—not the terms of the trust, not the beneficiaries, not even the assets.

3. To distribute wealth to inheriting parties according your predetermined timetable or qualifications.

TAXATION AT DEATH

The biggest threats to your wealth at death are the taxes your estate may owe. These taxes allow the government to generate revenue, and they prevent the wealthy from passing all of their assets to younger generations. It is important to note here that I have nothing against taxes. Governments provide us with valuable services using our tax dollars. What I'm talking about here in terms of wealth management planning is making sure that your estate doesn't owe more taxes than is absolutely required under the current tax laws. There are four taxes that can affect your wealth when you die:

Estate tax. It is unclear how the federal estate tax will change in the coming years. That's why I tell people to plan with today's tax rules in mind, and alter their plans in the future if the rules change. I must say that going forward, the odds are pretty good that some form of federal or state estate tax will be in place, and your estate will owe some form of estate tax when you die unless steps are taken to protect your wealth. What exactly comprises an estate, for estate tax purposes? You and your professional advisors need to perform a series of calculations to determine if your estate will owe estate taxes at death:

- **Step #1: Calculate your estate's gross value.** Your *gross estate* is equal to the total fair market value of, at death, assets you own solely and all property in which you owned an interest, and any asset you gifted to a descendent or trust within three years of death. So, your estate includes all property such as cars and jewelry, cash, securities, business interests, real estate, retirement plan assets, post-death employee benefits and life insurance benefits.

- **Step #2: Calculate your taxable estate.** To arrive at this figure, subtract the allowable federal deductions. These include:

  ➤ The unlimited marital deduction, which allows you to pass an unlimited amount of assets to your spouse.

  ➤ The charitable deduction, which allows you to subtract transfers at death to charities.

  ➤ Interest in stock ownership plans—if the transfer qualifies under the Internal Revenue Code 664(g).

  ➤ Funeral and estate administrative expenses.

  ➤ Claims against the estate.

  ➤ Debts, including unpaid mortgages.

  ➤ Losses suffered while settling the estate.

- **Step #3: Determine your tax base.** This is calculated by adding your taxable estate and all gifts you have given to individuals.

- **Step #4: Determine your tentative tax.** Apply the tax rate from the tax-rate table to your tax base.

- **Step #5: Take a gift tax reduction.** Avoid double taxation by subtracting all gift taxes paid from your tentative tax.

- **Step #6: Subtract any tax credits.** These include:

  > Unified estate and gift tax credit.

  > State estate tax credit.

  > Credit for estate taxes paid on transfers to the deceased person's estate.

  > Credit for estate taxes paid to a foreign government.

  > Credit for gift taxes paid.

- **Step #7:** The result is the amount that will face federal estate tax under the current tax law at rates of up to 46% in 2006 for the and up to 45% from 2007 through 2009. If your state imposes an estate tax of, say, 5%, you will have to add that additional tax to the federal tax to determine your total estate tax, which in our example would be 51%.

As you can see from this series of calculations, the size of your estate for estate tax purposes may be lower than expected. But as you also can see, the tax rates that are applied are staggeringly high, which means planning is essential. Without planning, nearly half of every dollar in your estate over the exemption amount that is not subject to a deduction will be removed for federal taxes. I tell people that rather than pay all of that money in estate taxes and let the government decide who will receive your money at death, why not plan and decide for yourself.

Gift tax. Gifts made outright to other individuals within three years of death, as well as the appreciated value of those gifts, are not included in your taxable estate. And any gift tax you may have paid on gifted property can be deducted from your estate. However, the value of a gifted asset will be brought back into your estate if you enjoyed the property, you had the right to access income from the property or controlled who possessed or enjoyed the property.

This problem turns up most often with life insurance policies. Typically, someone who is ill will transfer the policy to his or her children to prevent the benefit from entering his or her estate at death, thereby minimizing gift and estate taxes. But if the transfer was made within three years of death, the policy's value will be brought back into the person's estate for tax purposes—even though the insurance proceeds will still be paid to the children. This problem can cause a tax burden for the estate if there are not sufficient assets remaining in the estate to pay the tax.

A better solution might be to have the children buy the policy from the policy's owner for the cash value of the policy. If the policy's owner is in very poor health, the children can even get a loan to buy the policy if they do not have the money, since they can expect that death will bring a payout that will allow them to repay the loan. Consult your professional advisors about the steps needed to satisfy the IRS and minimize the risk of assets you gifted not being included in your estate.

Generation-skipping transfer tax. When you die, assets left directly to, or through a trust, to a grandchild (or any person not your spouse who is more than 37½ years younger than you) will face a generation-skipping transfer tax (GST) in addition to the estate tax. The IRS does not want you to *skip* a generation because it wants to be able to tax the wealth transfer at every generation. When there is a skip, the government loses an opportunity to tax the wealth transfer.

But there is an exception to the rule: There is no GST tax if the estate transfer is made to a grandchild when the child's parent on your side (your adult child) is deceased. This is because there is no child to *skip* over when the generation between the grandparent and the grandchild no longer exists. Instead, there is a direct transfer from grandparent to the grandchild.

Income tax of inherited property. Beneficiaries will owe income tax at their rate on trust distributions and on any inherited assets that they sell. The cost basis for income tax purposes usually is based on the fair market value at the time of inheritance.

SETTING UP A BYPASS TRUST

Now that you know how assets remaining in your estate at death will be taxed, you need to consider ways to minimize the most significant tax—the estate tax. Otherwise, your wealth could be significantly reduced.

Leaving all of your remaining assets to your spouse may seem like an efficient strategy. Under the unlimited marital deduction, there are no estate taxes on assets inherited by a spouse. The bad news is that your estate tax credit cannot be passed on to your spouse at death. You either use it or lose it. When your spouse dies, only his or her own estate tax exemption will be available to his or her estate. This means a greater portion of your spouse's estate (what was inherited plus his or her assets) could face steep estate taxes because they will not have the unlimited marital deduction to take advantage of.

To pass assets to your spouse and preserve your estate tax exclusion, you will need to write your will so that a bypass trust (also known as a *credit-shelter trust*) is established when you die. A bypass trust shelters assets in your estate equal to your estate tax exclusion—which could be significant. The bypass trust can distribute income, dividends and interest to your spouse during his or her lifetime, and your spouse can use the assets in the trust for your children's education, health and medical expenses.

When your spouse dies, the remaining assets are not considered part of his or her estate, so they avoid estate taxes, regardless of how much they may have appreciated over time. Instead, the assets pass to the trust's designated beneficiaries—normally your children and descendents. As a result, it's a good idea to have your wealth advisor continue to help your spouse invest the assets in the bypass trust so they can grow as much as possible over time.

If you have an estate of significant size, you will want to instruct that appreciated assets be placed in the trust. You also will need to draft the trust so that the trustee is instructed not to distribute income out of the bypass trust if other assets are available to the spouse from other sources. The goal is to have your spouse live off of the taxable assets in his or her estate rather than assets that have already been exempted from estate tax.

SETTING UP OTHER TRUSTS

Once you've set up a bypass trust to preserve your estate tax exclusion, you also need to consider establishing additional trusts through your will to ensure that other assets pass the way you intended and that inheriting children and descendents use the assets appropriately.

For this purpose, there are trusts that keep pools of inherited assets intact for a spouse, for children and descendents:

Qualified terminable interest property trust (QTIP). This trust is designed to support the surviving spouse, but it also ensures that your children or other descendents eventually inherit specific assets, such as real estate, that you left to your spouse.

As you now know, naming your spouse to inherit your assets at death will allow those assets to avoid estate taxes because of the unlimited marital deduction. Setting up a bypass trust will enable your estate tax exclusion to be preserved rather than lost. But what if you want your children to inherit a house that has been in your family a long time. This may be a potent issue in a second marriage. If your spouse remarries, there's always a chance that the house could pass to another person. For example, your spouse could leave everything he or she inherited to the new spouse or to children from the new marriage.

A QTIP trust solves this problem. All assets in a QTIP trust qualify for the unlimited marital deduction, so they escape estate tax. The independent trustee you named will manage the trust's assets for your spouse, and your spouse will receive annual income from the trust. Your spouse also can use the assets in the trust during his or her lifetime.

But when your spouse dies, the trust's designated beneficiary that you've named—a child, for example—will inherit the assets. In other words, your spouse cannot alter your original intention for those assets. You can, however, give the spouse the right to name the beneficiaries in his or her will from a select group of people, such as your children.

Why would you do this? There may be friction in the family, and you may want to be sure that the children look after the surviving spouse when you are gone. If the children know that the spouse has the ability to keep them out of the trust, they are more likely to be kind to the spouse and take care of the spouse to stay in his or her good graces.

Again, it's important to remember that jointly held assets you want to pass into a QTIP set up by your will must be solely owned or titled *tenants in common*—not *joint tenants with rights of survivorship*.

Qualified personal residence trust (QPRT). A QPRT lets you remove a valuable primary or secondary residence from your estate for tax purposes, but still allows your surviving spouse to use it. Here's how it works: When you die, the residence passes into a QPRT rather than passing directly to your surviving spouse. Your spouse is allowed to live in the house for a predetermined number of years. After that period, the house passes to the trust's designated beneficiaries, at which point, if your spouse is still alive, he or she can rent from the inheriting heirs.

Many couples use a QPRT for a vacation home instead of their primary residence because of the terms relating to the surviving spouse's stay in the house. These terms state that if the surviving spouse outlives the terms of free residence, he or she will have to pay a fair market rent to the beneficiaries who inherited the property through the trust. The problem here is that paying rent can be an uncomfortable arrangement for the surviving spouse, who once owned the house. Such a dilemma and discomfort doesn't usually exist with a vacation or second home.

Or you can designate a charity as the beneficiary of the trust. This strategy is especially useful for couples whose children do not wish to be burdened with the upkeep and/or sale of the property.

Again, the property must be solely owned or titled *tenants in common* to pass through your will and into the QPRT.

Charitable remainder trust (CRT). Assets gifted at death to an irrevocable CRT will make specific annual payments to the CRT's income beneficiary (such as the surviving spouse) over a specific period of time, based on an annuity payment schedule. After the time period elapses, the remaining assets in the CRT pass to charities named as remainder beneficiaries. There are both income and estate tax advantages of a CRT gift, so consult your wealth advisor and other financial professionals.

Qualified domestic trust (QDOT). A QDOT is set up when one spouse is a U.S. citizen but wants to leave property to a noncitizen spouse while qualifying for the unlimited marital deduction and preserving the estate tax credit through a bypass trust.

Otherwise your spouse could not inherit your assets tax-free. Why is this an issue for the IRS? Let's say you were married to a Canadian citizen. Without some type of trust in place, when you die, your spouse would inherit your assets tax-free. Let's say that your spouse then returns to Canada where he or she later dies. Your spouse would escape U.S. estate tax.

As a result, the IRS says that the only way a noncitizen spouse can qualify for the tax breaks is if your assets pass into a QDOT. Then your spouse can receive income from the trust on at least an annual basis. You also would designate the beneficiary who would receive the assets in the trust after your spouse dies, provided the beneficiary and trustee are U.S. citizens.

There's one more rule: A U.S. citizen or U.S. corporation must be named as the QDOT's trustee. In other words, you can't name a noncitizen spouse as the trustee of the QDOT trust. When your noncitizen spouse dies, the trustee will be responsible for ensuring that any estate tax due will be paid to the IRS in this country.

Irrevocable life insurance trust. This trust is established for a life insurance policy, and its purpose is to keep life insurance out of your estate so its death benefit proceeds will not be subject to estate tax when you die. In most cases, buying a policy inside the trust makes the most sense. This means you create the trust first and then make a cash donation to the trust to fund the premium payments for the policy. The policy is owned by the trust so it stays out of your estate. If you had bought the policy first and then put it in the trust, the policy would be brought back into your estate for estate tax purposes if you died within three years of the time the policy was put into the trust. Your spouse and an independent party can serve as co-trustees, and the trust's assets can be used by your surviving spouse for the care of your children and for basic living expenses. When your spouse dies, the remaining assets can pass directly to the trust's beneficiary or into another trust for lifetime distributions.

PROTECTING YOUR MAJOR ASSETS

Many assets that remain in your estate at death—such as taxable market securities and cash—are relatively easy to pass to your spouse or divide among your children and descendents in accordance with your will or beneficiary forms. Other assets such as a family business, retirement plans and real estate are often more significant in value and more complex, requiring careful advance planning to ensure tax efficiency and wealth preservation.

Family businesses. During your lifetime, you and your wealth advisor and other financial professionals should regularly review and discuss who will succeed you in the event of your death. You also will need to devote time and effort to grooming the family members you've chose to become owner and manager. They will likely need personal management coaching as well as hands-on experience so they can handle the leadership and finance issues that are critical to business success. Otherwise there is likely to be discord among surviving family members over the parties who succeed you as owner and manager. In my experience, such discord over the owners and managers of a family-owned business after death almost always leads to costly delays, lost opportunities, turmoil and, in some cases, a forced sale or bankruptcy.

When selecting a successor owner, you need to be sure that the person is truly knowledgeable about running the business and not just the best possible alternative among family members. That person also should have his or her heart in the enterprise. Once this person has been selected, you need to invest time helping to educate and polish that person's skills. You also need to give them plenty of opportunities to fail and handle crises.

In so many cases, an heir is selected to be the successor owner because he or she has the best relationship with the parent owner—but little is done to train the heir apparent or put that person into real-world situations. Likewise, if your successor owner is a trust created for the benefit of the nonbusiness family members, you need to know whether the trustee can handle the task, and train the trustee to handle the challenges he or she is likely to face.

Taxes also represent a major hurdle for a family-owned business when the owner dies. Upon death, if your business is to pass directly into the hands of successor owners, there are often transfer taxes due. Your wealth advisors, accountant and attorney may need to use special formulas to determine the value of your business. For example, certain real estate owned by your business can be valued based on its *actual use* rather than its *best possible use*, which can be a more beneficial calculation.

When valuing a business, the goal always is to seek the lowest possible assessment for tax purposes. For example, there are two ways to accomplish this based on whether the business will continue to operate or whether it will be sold. There also are ways to restructure the ownership of the business to reduce the valuation of the part remaining in your estate at death.

A closely held company can pay its share of taxes and expense without incurring the dividend treatment of a normal corporate distribution. Ideally, you'll want to fix the value of the company for tax purposes and assign the appreciation to another individual. One way to do this is through corporate recapitalization, which requires a reorganization of the company's capital structure. In addition, while federal estate taxes are due within nine months after a person dies, there are tax codes that allow for deferred installment payments when certain requirements and conditions are met.

Your accountant and other financial professionals will be able to provide you with strategies for passing property to responsible heirs.

Retirement plans. At death, assets remaining in your 401(k) and IRA pass to the party you named as primary beneficiary. There are special rights and rules regarding these assets and your surviving spouse. There also are rules that relate to estate taxes, gift taxes and the generation-skipping transfer taxes that will need to be studied and addressed by your wealth advisors. Remember, these assets are included as part of your taxable estate before they pass to those you've named as beneficiaries. Gifts of these plans' assets to charitable causes at death usually will qualify your estate for an estate tax charitable deduction and allow these assets to avoid taxation.

Real estate. Leaving real estate to your children and descendents may sound simple, but properties are not easily divided or shared. For example, children who inherit homes often battle over the times of year when their families can use the house. They also feud over who should pay for the house's upkeep and renovation. And they typically have large disagreements about when to sell and for how much.

These decisions are often based on the needs of each child's family, and their income and financial standing. Your wealth advisor and accountant can inform you about tax strategies to reduce or freeze the values of your real estate holdings, the discounts that apply when properties are fractionally owned, special use valuations and qualified personal residence trusts.

1. Identify all assets likely to be in your estate at death.

2. Ask your accountant to calculate the tax impact of those remaining assets on your estate. Taxes include the estate tax, gift tax and generation-skipping transfer tax—and any income-tax implications for heirs.

3. Discuss with your accountant and estate attorney strategies for minimizing these taxes and preserving wealth.

4. Consider establishing a bypass trust through your will to preserve your estate tax credit at death.

5. Consider setting up survivor's trusts to minimize estate taxes and control how heirs receive and use inherited assets.

6. Retitle assets where necessary so assets pass according to updated estate plans.

7. Ask your financial professionals to recommend tax-efficient inheritance strategies for complex assets such as a family business, retirement plans and real estate.

13

IMPLEMENTING CHARITABLE INCLINATIONS AT DEATH

Individuals who choose to leave assets to charity when they die typically do so for a combination of factors: they want to give back to their community, they feel that they have already provided family with a sufficient inheritance, and they want to significantly reduce the size of their taxable estate by qualifying for a dollar-for-dollar estate tax deduction.

But there's another big benefit to donating assets remaining in your estate to charity at death —the opportunity to leave your family with what I call a *value legacy*. By setting up a pool of funds—such as a private family foundation, donor advised fund or a charitable family limited partnership—during your lifetime or at death, and donating assets to the pool when you die, you can involve your family in a charitable mission that can extend beyond your lifetime and theirs.

Gifting assets tax-efficiently to charity at death and enlisting your family's participation requires careful planning. Otherwise, there's greater risk that more taxes will be owed by your estate than necessary and that family members will lack the financial skills necessary to oversee charitable assets or manage their own inherited wealth.

But let me be clear: I am not suggesting you take steps while you're alive to ensure that family members manage charitable assets wisely after you die so you can become a control freak from the grave. Whenever I talk to audiences on this topic, I can see from the expressions on their faces that they're asking themselves why they should bother making a fuss about events that are going to take place after they're gone.

By the time I finish talking, however, people who never thought about gifting assets to charity at death usually come rushing up to me to say they weren't aware of the substantial wealth-preserving and family-bonding benefits of doing so.

At the very least, think of your family's involvement as a way to protect your charitable investments. Donating assets to charity is an act of generosity, but not all charities use gifts wisely and, in some cases, charities that are well managed today can wind up being mismanaged in the future. Giving your family members control over assets intended for charities, instead of making gifts directly to charities at your death, allows family members to play an ongoing role in evaluating the charities that will receive the assets over time.

In this chapter I will show you how to pass estate assets tax-efficiently to charity and involve your family gracefully in the charitable process, which will ensure that your charitable goals are met and that your family learns valuable lessons about finance, giving and harmony.

CHARITABLE GIFTING AND TAXES

To encourage charitable gifting, the IRS provides significant tax breaks for donations made either during your lifetime or at death. As a result, charitable bequests of assets from your estate at your death not only assist charitable causes, but also preserves more of your wealth for surviving family members by reducing the taxes your estate will owe. Here is a brief review of the tax rules as they relate to charitable donations:

Income taxes. The type of assets you chose to donate to charity during your lifetime and the type of charity you choose to support will determine the extent of your income tax deduction. Cash gifts to a public charity are permitted the full 50% deduction, while cash gifts to a private charity can claim only a 30% deduction. Gifts of appreciated assets—such as market securities and real estate—receive a 30% deduction when donated to a public charity but only 20% when donated to a private charity. For tax deduction purposes, a private family foundation is considered a private charity, while a donor managed investment account is considered a public charity.

Estate taxes. Gifts to charity at death are 100% deductible for estate tax purposes, meaning your estate receives a dollar-for-dollar estate tax deduction. As a result, a charitable donation at death can significantly lower the size of your estate, and the more you give away at death to charity, the less will be sitting in your estate when the IRS comes to collect its estate taxes.

MAKING GIFTS TAX-EFFICIENTLY

In my experience, people who give assets to charity at death have already taken steps to provide for their spouse and children. In other words, the excess remaining in their estate is what is passed to charity. But the definition of *excess* varies from individual to individual. Some people purposefully want their children to inherit as little as possible for fear that too much wealth will corrupt their children's work ethic, undermine their drive to be successful, or blunt their sensitivity toward people who have much less. Others would rather provide assets to their children during their lifetimes and gift what remains at death.

As you can see, your decision to donate assets at death to charity will depend on your views about wealth, family dynamics and giving. How much to give typically starts by accurately projecting the estate tax your estate will likely owe at death. Then you will need to work though different gifting scenarios to find the one that best meets your goals. Here are key questions to consider:

- How much do you want to gift?
- Which charities do you want to receive the gift?
- Do you want to make an outright gift or involve your family in gifting over time?
- How will your intended gift affect your taxable estate?
- Have you accounted for your family's inheritance needs?

Once you have calculated the size of your taxable estate—updating this information annually—and have resolved the big questions listed above with your financial professionals, you need to determine which assets to gift at death to charity and which to bequeath to your family. Ultimately, different assets will have different tax implications on your estate.

GIFTING YOUR RETIREMENT PLANS

One of the biggest estate planning mistakes affluent people make is leaving assets outside of retirement plans to charity and leaving their IRA and 401(k) or other qualified retirement plan (QRP) assets to a spouse, children or descendents. Their logic is that by gifting nonretirement-plan assets to charity, the size of their taxable estate will be reduced and the timely and costly probate process will be avoided. And by passing retirement-plan assets to family members, those who inherit the assets will be able to extend the tax-favored status of these accounts over their longer lifetimes.

Sounds smart, but doing the exact opposite actually is more tax-efficient. Here's why: If you leave nonretirement-plan appreciated assets to family members, these assets will receive a step-up in cost basis at your death. That means if a building you bought 20 years ago for $800,000 is worth $6 million when you die, your family members who inherit the building won't owe capital gain taxes if they sell the building for $6 million—their stepped-up cost basis.

By contrast, if they inherit your IRA, the IRA will be considered part of your taxable estate and your estate will owe estate tax on the account's value if your estate qualifies for taxation. In addition, annual withdrawals (mandatory or otherwise) from the IRA by inheriting family members will be taxed as ordinary income at their personal income tax rate.

If your IRA is hit with a 50% state and federal estate tax and then a 40% state and federal income tax, more than 70 cents of every dollar in the IRA will go to pay a tax, leaving very little for your family. This is terrible!

Instead, by leaving appreciated assets to descendents and leaving retirement-plan assets to charity, you will be passing wealth more tax-efficiently. Descendents will receive a step-up in basis and wind up inheriting a significantly larger percentage of your net wealth. And by gifting retirement-plan assts to charity, you will dramatically reduce the size of your taxable estate and allow the charity to receive the full value of those accounts, free of taxes.

Of course, this strategy depends on the value of your retirement-plan assets, the value of assets not held in retirement plans and your family's financial needs. That's why it's essential to discuss this decision carefully with your wealth advisor and other financial professionals.

Setting Up Charitable Trusts

A charitable trust can be set up during your lifetime to receive your assets at death or the trust can be set up at death through your will to receive the assets. Depending on the type of charitable trust you establish, the assets can benefit both your descendents and charities while providing your estate with significant tax savings.

Why use a charitable trust? You may want to make charitable gifts at death for tax or personal reasons without shortchanging family members who need income or assets. Here's how the most common charitable trusts work *(for more detailed information on these trusts, see Chapter 9):*

Charitable remainder trusts (CRT). Assets are donated to the CRT at your death, and income from the trust is paid to the trust's designated income beneficiary for a set period of years or for the lifetime of the beneficiary (such as for the lifetime of your spouse). The charity you've named as remainder beneficiary will take control of the donated asset when the last income beneficiary dies or the trust term ends. The trustee maintains full investment control of the assets in the CRT.

There are two types of CRTs—a charitable remainder annuity trust (CRAT) and a charitable remainder unitrust (CRUT). In a CRAT, your donated assets fund a fixed annual annuity payment to the designated income beneficiaries. In a CRUT, the assets provide annual annuity payments on a variable basis, meaning the payment will fluctuate depending the value of the asset.

Charitable lead trusts (CLT). This type of trust works like the charitable remainder trust—but in reverse. Assets that are transferred into the CLT must pay income to one or more charities over a set period of time. When that period ends, the trust's designated beneficiaries (your family members) will receive the trust's assets.

There are two types of CLTs—a charitable lead annuity trust (CLAT) and a charitable lead unitrust (CLUT). In a CLAT, income is paid to the charity based on a fixed rate. In a CLUT, income is paid at a variable rate based on the value of the donated assets.

Some people who direct that their remaining assets pass into a charitable trust when they die still want their spouse or descendents to receive the equivalent value of those assets to live on. In such cases, these donors typically use an asset-replacement strategy involving life insurance when they create the charitable giving plan.

Here's how it works: An irrevocable life insurance trust is set up outside of the estate, which then purchases a life insurance policy on the life of the person making the asset donation at death. Family members are named beneficiaries of the policy.

At the donor's death, assets are transferred to charity based on the donor's wishes, reducing the size of the estate for estate tax purposes. The value of the assets gifted will then be replaced by the life insurance proceeds in the life insurance trust. Since these assets are outside of the estate, they escape estate tax, and the life insurance trust can pay assets to the family members as directed by the donor in the trust document. Ask your wealth advisor and other financial advisors to explain how life insurance can be used to replace the value of assets donated to charity at death.

LEAVING A VALUE LEGACY

Up until now I've told you about the most tax-efficient ways to donate assets remaining in your estate directly to charities, or indirectly by donating them to a charitable trust. An outright gift at death prevents you or your family from having any control over how the assets are used. And while a charitable trust provides family members with annual income or the trust's principal, family members will play no collective role in managing the assets or distributing them to charity after your death.

If you have children, descendents, grandchildren or nieces or nephews, there is a way to engage them in the charitable process—and leave them and future generations with a *value legacy*. By donating estate assets to a pool of funds—either a private family foundation, donor managed investment account or charitable family limited partnership—your family members play a role in the future of those assets.

Three big goals will be accomplished when you set up a pool of funds:

- Family members will learn the joy of gifting and other values they can pass on to their own children.

- Family members will learn about finance—lessons they will be able to use when managing their own finances.

- Family members will be compelled to unite at least annually to bond and discuss the pool's affairs.

TAX BENEFITS OF FUND POOLS

Assets donated at death to a private family foundation, donor managed investment account, or charitable family limited partnership provides many tax benefits and family advantages:

Private family foundation. You set up a private family foundation (PPF) to receive your donated assets. A PPF also gives trustees (your family members and others) complete control over how donated assets are managed, which charities will receive them and how much each charity will receive each year.

Family trustees must meet regularly, and a PPF must distribute at least 5% of its assets each year to public charities. The PPF is responsible for the cost and staffing of all back-office duties, which include producing a comprehensive valuation of appreciated assets donated to the foundation. Keeping careful records of board meetings, and accounting records, are essential for tax purposes. Given the cost to set up and manage a PPF on an ongoing basis, a PPF often is most ideal for sizable estates. Assets in your estate when you die that are given to a PPF qualify for a dollar-for-dollar charitable estate tax deduction.

If you want family members to receive the equivalent value of assets donated to a PPF, consider establishing an irrevocable life insurance trust and purchasing a life insurance policy naming family members as beneficiaries. Or set up a legacy trust, which avoids estate taxes for up to three generations. A legacy trust places assets outside your estate and the reach of creditors, legal judgments, malpractice suits and divorcing spouses. Once you have funded the legacy trust with assets during your lifetime, children and descendents would receive a lump sum when you pass away. Or the trust could provide for grandchildren or great-grandchildren. The assets are 100% free of estate tax and the generation-skipping transfer tax.

Or you could combine a PPF with a charitable remainder trust. This arrangement would allow family members to receive income for life from the trust and earn tax savings, while maintaining control of the assets you do-nated to the PPF.

Donor managed investment account (DMI). A DMI gives your family members the ability to manage the assets you contributed irrevocably to a charity dur-ing your lifetime. Here's how it works: You create a DMI account at a charity and contribute assets during your lifetime or at death. The assets are held in an account at a financial institution of your choosing. Then you and the charity sign a *gift agreement* that gives you and your heirs the power to man-age the investment of donated assets for a set period. The charity will assume control of the assets at the end of the term or when the assets drop in value by a predetermined percentage. Donations at death qualify for a charitable estate tax deduction.

Back-office tasks are handled for a nominal fee by the institution managing the assets, and the DMI must distribute at least 5% of its assets each year.

The equivalent value of assets donated to the DMI can be passed to family members through a legacy trust or irrevocable life insurance trust.

Charitable family limited partnership (CFLP). A CFLP allows you to make a significant gift to charity during your lifetime and at death. A CFLP also provides income tax deductions, reduces the size of your taxable estate, and gives some family members influence over how the assets are used.

Here's how it works: In a CFLP there are *general partners* who control the operation of the CFLP and make investment decisions, and *limited partners* who share the profits but have no control over the CFLP. By naming you and your spouse (or even other family members) general partners, your fam-ily will decide after you die who will receive the limited partner shares. In practice, general partners transfer a small portion of the limited partnership shares to children and the bulk to one or more charities. The general part-ners claim a charitable income tax deduction for the fair market value of the limited partnership interests given to the charity.

Assets donated to the CFLP at your death will provide the limited partners with a share of the income. Eventually, the CFLP sells the appreciated assets, enabling the charity to receive its portion of the gain while the remaining pro-ceeds are reinvested by the CFLP. As a result, most of the gain escapes taxation because the charity owns most of the limited partnership shares. After a set period of time, the CFLP liquidates, and the charity receives its share of the reinvested assets while your descendents receive their share. A CFLP is ideal for assets such as closely held stock, real estate or a family business.

A charity also can be given a *put*, which is the right to require the CFLP to buy its limited partnership shares after a set period of time. The price of these shares can be discounted by the CFLP for tax purposes because the shares lack marketability, the charity has no management control and the charity is liquidating its interest before the CFLP's term expires. The assets that remain in the CFLP will then belong to the other limited partners, usually your children. The discount allows greater wealth to be transferred to your children without owing gift or estate tax.

A CFLP gives the general partners greater control over how to invest donated assets and which charities will receive limited partnership shares.

INFORMING HEIRS OF CHARITABLE PLANS

Whatever plans you put in place to donate assets to charity at death, I'm a firm believer in letting children know about them. Such conversations between you, your wealth advisor and your children help them understand what you're doing and let them realize the good you are trying to accomplish. Some individuals prefer not to disclose their plans, fearing that their children will become resentful about not inheriting as much as they would have wished. In my experience, much of the anger children feel when they hear of a parent's charitable plans at death can be eased or erased by setting up entities while you're alive that involve them in the decision-making process.

Set up correctly, these entities may even be able to pay for family gatherings, which could be held in a fun place. Each child can present his or her recommendation for a charitable cause to benefit each year, and the group researches the charity prior to donation and then votes. You can even write a letter of instruction outlining your charitable ambitions and wishes for your family gatherings. Such a letter might say, "I want all of you to be aware of causes in the community, the city, the state and the nation. And I want you to get together once a year with your siblings and decide how to give away the wealth we've set aside for charity. You are the stewards of those assets, and I want you to decide which causes we will benefit. I also want you to involve your children, so they understand the meaning of gifting and experience the joys gifting brings to others."

If financial professionals and family members manage the assets you donate to a pool of funds wisely, those assets should grow and last long into the future, continuing to do good for heirs and charities.

CHECKLIST

1. Calculate the size of your taxable estate with your financial professionals.

2. Determine the tax benefits of gifting specific assets during life and at death.

3. Select charities you want to receive the assets.

4. Consider setting up a charitable trust if you want heirs to receive income or the principal.

5. Consider a private family foundation, donor managed investment account to involve family members in your charitable mission.

6. Set up a legacy trust or irrevocable life insurance trust if you want family to be able to replace the value of assets donated to charity.

7. Take steps to be sure your family fully understands your charitable motives and what will be required of them if you plan to set up a pool of funds.

8. Involve your financial professionals in laying the groundwork and training for family participation in charitable gifting.

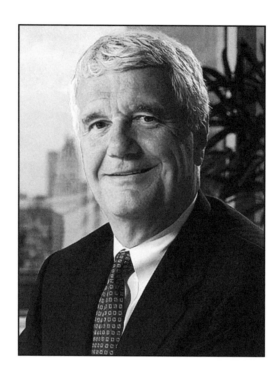

TED RIDLEHUBER is president and CEO of the Cannon Financial Institute in Athens, Ga., one of the country's largest providers of training and certification programs for private wealth advisors. Ted Ridlehuber began his career as a trusts and estates attorney, and has served on the boards of several banks. As a private wealth management consultant, he helps affluent families maximize their wealth potential and advises the majority of the nation's best-known financial institutions on the needs of the high-net-worth marketplace.

Ted Ridlehuber is available for public speaking engagements and informational events on the 13 wealth management topics covered in this book. Contact the Cannon Financial Institute at (888) 353-3346.

www.CannonFinancial.com